Foreign Policy of India in Southeast Asia

Foreign Policy of India in Southeast Asia

Edited by

Josukutty C.A.

Associate Professor and Honorary Director,
Survey Research Centre, Department of Political Science,
University of Kerala.

New Century Publications
New Delhi, India

NEW CENTURY PUBLICATIONS
4800 / 24, Bharat Ram Road,
Ansari Road, Daryaganj,
New Delhi - 110 002 (India)

Tel.: 011-2324 7798, 4358 7398, 4101 7798

E-mail: info@newcenturypublications.com

www.newcenturypublications.com

Editorial Office:
4832/24, Ansari Road, Daryaganj,
New Delhi – 110 002

Tel.: 011-4356 0919

First Published: **2020**

ISBN: **978-81-7708-500-6**

Published by New Century Publications and printed at Milan Enterprises, New Delhi.

Designs: Patch Creative Unit, New Delhi.

PRINTED IN INDIA

About the Book

India's historical and cultural relations with Southeast Asia have the potential to realize security and strategic purposes. The earliest sustained contact between India and Southeast Asia was through Southern and Eastern coastal states of India during the Chola and Kalinga empires. If connection through the North-Eastern states is vital for economic development of the region, integration through the Southern and Eastern coastal states of India is crucial for the promotion of larger maritime security and strategic interests. The ports and naval bases in Southern and Eastern coastal India and the strategic locations of the Bay of Bengal and Andaman and Nicobar Islands are of vital significance. Despite having one of the largest merchant fleets in the developing world, Indian ports have a limited number of direct calls with ASEAN ports.

The biggest challenge for India in the region is managing its relationship with China. China's assertiveness in maritime territorial disputes in South China Sea and expanding presence in East Asia and the Indian Ocean has reinforced the relevance of an enhanced role for India and its Asia-Pacific partners in these regions.

The present volume contains 8 scholarly papers that discuss various dimensions of India's foreign policy in Southeast Asia.

Editor's Profile

Dr. Josukutty C.A. is currently Associate Professor and Honorary Director, Survey Research Centre, Department of Political Science, University of Kerala. He received his M.A. (Political Science), M.Phil. and Ph.D. degrees from the University of Kerala, India. He was a fellow of the Salzburg Global Seminar, 2007. He was selected to study U.S. foreign policy at the University of Florida in 2010.

Dr. Josukutty was awarded the Fulbright Nehru Academic and Professional Excellence Fellowship in 2015. He has to his credit four books and more than sixty research and popular articles. He has been serving as General Secretary, Association of Political Scientists, Kerala since 2011. His areas of interest and research include international relations, India's foreign policy, Indo-U.S. relations, electoral politics, and human rights.

Contents

Contributors

Mohanan Bhaskaran Pillai	Head, Department of Politics and International Studies, Pondicherry University, Puducherry.
S. Utham Kumar Jamadhagni	Associate Professor, Department of Defence and Strategic Studies, University of Madras, Chennai, Tamil Nadu.
Asma Masood	Research Officer; Programme Director-Internships, Chennai Centre for China Studies, Chennai, Tamil Nadu.
J. Susanna Lobo	Doctoral Candidate, Department of Political Science, University of Delhi, Delhi.
Rose Veera D Souza	Head, Department of Political Science, St. Aloysius College, Mangaluru, Karnataka.
Tran Ngoc Diem	Department of International Relation Studies, Institute for Indian and Southwest Asian Studies, Vietnam Academy of Social Sciences, Ha Noi, Vietnam.
Gayathry Gopal	Research Scholar, SIS, Jawaharlal Nehru University (JNU), New Delhi.
Suresh K.	Assistant Professor, Department of Political Science, Government College, Kattappana, Kerala.

Introduction by the Editor

India's historical and cultural relations with the region have the potential to realize security and strategic purposes. The earliest sustained contact between India and Southeast Asia was through Southern and Eastern coastal states of India during the Chola and Kalinga empires. If connection through the North-Eastern states is vital for economic development of the region, integration through the Southern and Eastern coastal states of India is crucial for the promotion of larger maritime security and strategic interests. The ports and naval bases in South and Eastern coastal India and the strategic location of the Bay of Bengal and Andaman and Nicobar Islands are of vital significance. It is noteworthy that despite having one of the largest merchant fleets in the developing world, Indian ports have a limited number of direct calls with the ASEAN ports.

The biggest challenge for India in the region is managing its relationship with China. China's assertiveness in maritime territorial disputes in South China Sea and expanding presence in East Asia and the Indian Ocean including South Asia has reinforced the relevance of an enhanced role for India and its Asia-Pacific partners in these regions. As China's relationship with India's neighbours in the Indian Ocean deepens, the strategic relevance of India's own connections with neighbouring Asian states in the Indo-Pacific Ocean needs to be strengthened.

This has assumed greater significance in the context of the Belt and Road Initiative as it demands well thought out plans on the Indian side to balance China economically, geopolitically and strategically. Relations between India and China would not only decide the future of the Indo-Pacific region, but also the global world order of the 21st century and India's place in it. The critical question is how India can simultaneously promote its vital national interests to become a major power and ensure peace in the region.

The present volume contains 8 scholarly papers that discuss various aspects and dimensions of India's foreign policy in Southeast Asia.

Mohanan Bhaskaran Pillai in his paper titled *India's Multi-vectored Alignment in the East: Aims, Objectives and Rationale* argues that 'Act East Policy' is India's response to the emerging multipolar world order within the ambit of the country's strategic doctrine. According to him, the bipolar international system of Cold War period produced India's nonalignment and the post-Cold War period of 'unipolar moment', marked by the collapse of the Soviet Union, led to the launch of 'Look East Policy'. In the course of the paper he examines the factors that determined the shaping of India's foreign policy during the Cold War period, the drivers of 'Look East Policy', the reasons for its rechristening into 'Act East Policy' and India's quest to emerge as a power of consequence in the multipolar world.

The paper titled *India-ASEAN Institutional Partnership in Maritime Security* by S. Utham Kumar Jamadhagni underlines the importance of maritime security for the successful implementation of 'Act East Policy'. Maritime security is vital in the institutionalisation of linkages between Indian and ASEAN countries. The paper reviews the advantage that has been garnered in this field in the past but more importantly the future possibilities it holds for congruity of interests for India and ASEAN.

Asma Masood's paper *India-ASEAN Civilizational and Cultural Links* probes the ancient cultural relations between India and ASEAN countries. India's civilizational presence in most of the ASEAN countries has religious, social, cultural and even royal fabrics. Today, these aspects form the basis for modern era linkages that are seen in tourism, spirituality, education and Diaspora. The paper examines how India can leverage its advantages of historical, civilizational and cultural ties with Southeast Asia to balance Chinese influence in the region and reap maximum mutual benefit for India and ASEAN in the coming decades.

The paper titled *Balancing China: India's Growing Presence in Southeast Asia* by J. Susanna Lobo employs the *balancing of power* theory to analyse India's growing presence in the Southeast Asian region by keeping New Delhi's two objectives in sight: first, to counterbalance China's relative power in the Asian region; and second, to respond to Beijing's strategic encirclement of India in the South Asia region to cap its prospects to grow beyond the region.

The author states that since the beginning of the 21st Century, India and the Southeast Asian states are concerned about China's power and its growing assertiveness in the maritime disputes. For this reason, their interests converge against the rising collective Chinese threat which, in turn, increases India's prospects to emerge as a long-term regional balancer. Against this backdrop, along with its economic relations, India has enhanced its defence and strategic ties with key Southeast Asian states. In short, the paper analyses the scope and prospects of India's balancing strategy against China in the Southeast Asian region with the help of regional and extra-regional powers.

The paper titled *Deepening of Relationship between India and South Korea* by Rose Veera D Souza focuses on the current relations between India and South Korea viz., economic relations, trade, investments, industrial know-how, strategic partnership, and energy security. Secondly, it edges on the efforts that India has taken to establish bilateral relations and in promoting sustained policies to act in this direction. Third, it attempts to unravel the nuances of security equations vis-à-vis *rising China*. The paper explains the trajectory of deepening bilateral relations between the two and the forthcoming trends it displays.

In the paper tilted *Promoting Vietnam-India Comprehensive Strategic Partnership*, Tran Ngoc Diem analyzes the impact of the 'Act East Policy' on bilateral cooperation and explores prospective directions for Vietnam-India relations in the future. The paper affirms that Vietnam and India possess a number of historical, international and regional advantages and the growing connectivity in political security, trading and investment, energy and culture would enable them to strengthen the comprehensive strategic relationship further.

Gayathry Gopal's paper titled *China in Maldives: India's Concerns* underlines the rising geopolitics in the Indian Ocean Region and increased competition from China. Both India and China compete for greater leverage in the Indian Ocean. Maldives is of critical strategic importance to India. India has enjoyed good relations with this neighbour in the past. But the rising influence of China and increasing radicalisation of Maldivian society is of much concern for India.

Through loans, grants and foreign direct investment, Beijing has made a heavy impact in Maldives. Maldives joining China's One Belt One Road project and the signing of the Free Trade Agreement with China are of great strategic significance. China's increasing assertiveness and an expanding geostrategic space coupled with cultural ties and a possible debt trap might push Maldives into China's security net. This would adversely impact the central goals of 'Act East Policy', boosting India's regional power and counter weighing the strategic influence of China.

The paper titled *Seeking Partnership with Taiwan: India's Big Power Ambitions* by Suresh K. evaluates the role and strategic significance of Taiwan in India's 'Act East Policy' and how it figures in India's big power ambitions in the long-run. India considers Taiwan an effective balancer against the growing influence of China in the region. At the same time, the author warns that using Taiwan as a strategic card may create instability in the region, which will ultimately harm both India and China.

I take this opportunity to express my gratitude and thanks to all the scholars who have contributed to this volume and enriched the literature on the India's foreign policy.

Thiruvananthapuram **Josukutty C.A.**

1

India's Multi-vectored Alignment in the East: Aims, Objectives, and Rationale

Mohanan Bhaskaran Pillai

India has emerged victorious in being part of many multilateral, regional and bilateral engagements of politico-strategic, economic and cultural importance in East Asia ever since the launching of the 'Look East Policy' (LEP) in 1992 in the wake of the collapse of the bipolar international system. In November 2014, Narendra Modi rechristened the ongoing engagement as 'Act East Policy' (AEP).

Does AEP signify more than just a name change? If so, what are the variables/drivers that contributed to such renaming of an ongoing policy? The argument is that both LEP and AEP are by-products of two distinct phases of unfolding contemporary history. The bipolar international system of Cold War period produced India's nonalignment and the post-Cold War period of 'unipolar moment' marked by the collapse of the Soviet Union led to the launching of LEP.

Many scholars of international relations observed and documented the fading away of the unipolar moment and the emergence of the multipolar international system and power configuration. This paper argues that AEP is India's response to the emerging multipolar world order within the ambit of the country's strategic doctrine.

Prime Minister Narendra Modi on November 12, 2014, at the 12th ASEAN-India summit and on the platform of the 9th East Asia Summit in Myanmar rechristened the ongoing engagement of India with the East Asian countries as 'Act East Policy' (AEP). Modi's state visits to Mongolia, Japan, China, and South Korea energised the efforts in elevating those engagements to a higher level by bringing in North-East Asia also into the framework of AEP. The extent to which East Asian partnerships are close to the heart of India's foreign policy priorities, got demonstrated by the unprecedented act of inviting the heads of states of all the 10 ASEAN countries as guests at the 69th Republic Day celebrations in New Delhi.

It appears that Modi's AEP is a definite shift without rupturing its organic link with the 'Look East Policy' (LEP) launched in 1992 under the premiership of Narasimha Rao in the wake of the collapse of the bipolar international system. LEP was initiated to reorient India's foreign economic policy in the post-Cold War era when India was reeling under a balance of payment crisis in the aftermath of the Gulf war and also due to the collapse of India's principal economic partner and political friend, the Soviet Union.

The Indian objective in keeping ASEAN, as the gateway to its East Asian engagements, was part of the attempt to get rehabilitated into the orbit of the unipolar world order. India wanted to befriend Southeast Asian countries with which the country maintained a safe distance during the height of the Cold War because India's nonalignment was not compatible with the clear anti-communist stance of the original five founding members of the ASEAN.

The LEP initiatives in the foreign economic policy of India coincided with the economic reforms of liberalisation, privatisation and globalisation and signalled the abandonment of the hitherto practised economic model of import substitution industrialisation as implemented in the post-independent India. The crux of the new initiative was embracing economic liberalism with the adoption of the export-led growth model (Shivkumar and Delgado, 2011, p. 110). Thus, LEP symbolised India's economic opening, new business opportunities and drawing inspiration from the success stories of the tiger economies of Southeast Asia. Originally conceived as an economic agenda to get integrated into the neo-liberal world economy through the gateway of ASEAN, it subsequently spilt over into cultural and strategic domains. Modi's AEP was intended to reactivate India's eastern engagement in the context of the country's assessment of capabilities vis-à-vis China and the US as also China's assertiveness in the region and US gradual disengagement in Asia-Pacific.

It is worth noting that India has completed 26 years of dialogue, 16 years of summit-level meetings and five years of strategic partnership with ASEAN–the core of India's multilevel engagement in the East. In 1992, ASEAN made India, a dialogue partner for a few sectors in its cooperation framework. Subsequently, in 1995, India became a full dialogue partner of ASEAN. In the next year, India got admission into the ASEAN post-ministerial conference and became a member in ASEAN Regional Forum (ARF).

India inked free trade agreement in goods and investments in 2009 and FTA in services and investments in 2014. India's multilevel engagement with ASEAN consists of 30 sectoral dialogue mechanisms, seven ministerial-level interactions in fields such as external affairs, defence, connectivity, commerce, telecommunications, agriculture, energy, environmental issues and tourism.

Additionally, India maintains strong bilateral bonds with each one of the ASEAN member states. In 1997, India initiated the sub-regional association called BIMSTEC. In 2000, India sponsored the Mekong-Ganga project between India and five ASEAN member countries to promote education, tourism and culture in the sub-region. Geographically, East Asia is close to India since the country shares land borders with Myanmar and Thailand and sea borders with Myanmar, Thailand as also with Malaysia and Singapore. More than a thousand years recorded history speaks about the trading relationships between Indian and some of the East Asian countries. This thousand-year history of mutual interaction has had its imprint on the language, religion and culture of the region. LEP, it seems, considered this aspect while launching the policy. Also, the perception was that the Indian Diaspora could play a meaningful role in strengthening India's new economic policy and its rehabilitation into the market-driven economy. Moreover, turbulent West Asia was not a viable route to get integrated into the neo-liberal political economy. The rise of China had also been taken into consideration while framing this 'Look East Policy'.

Now the question is whether AEP is a complete departure from LEP or not? What are the variables/drivers that contributed to such a renaming of an ongoing policy? What are the new variables added?

India's LEP and AEP have received scholarly attention from far and wide. Most of the studies have highlighted the economic imperatives of LEP/AEP (Ahmed, 2014). Its strategic dimension has also received adequate attention. Also, scholars have identified the systemic drivers and underlying factors of LEP/AEP (Muni, 2012); (Naidu, 2004); (Palit, 2010); (Sikri, 2009). Most of the studies have found in AEP/LEP, an effort from the side of India to balance China with active engagement with ASEAN grouping, Japan and South Korea. India's role as a balancer or 'swing state' requires more in-depth scholarly attention. At the same time, some Chinese scholars are of the view that both China and India loathe US hegemony in Asia and enough elbow room is available for the rise of both without entering into a competition mode (Hong, 2007).

Thus, the economic imperative and strategic aspects have received extensive scholarly attention. However, systematic analysis of contemporary history and the dynamics of international political economy as the contributing factor of LEP/AEP warrant detailed investigation. We would argue that right from the days of independence, the country's civilizational personality and the ambition to emerge as a country of consequence on the strength of civilizational continuum determined its foreign policy behaviour. In other words, both LEP and AEP are by-products of two distinct phases of unfolding contemporary history and the underlying factor is India's quest for recognition as a leading power, a desire ingrained in the collective Indian psyche as shaped by the legacy of its civilisation or the understanding and interpretation of Indian civilisation by the founding fathers of the Indian Republic.

Even a cursory look at contemporary history since independence would provide exciting insights into the above argument; the bipolar international system of Cold War period produced India's nonalignment and the post-Cold War period of 'unipolar moment' marked by the collapse of Soviet Union compelled India to look towards East. On a similar line, we would argue that AEP is one of the by-products of the emerging multipolar international system as understood and abstracted by Indian policy elite. The multipolar world order with a leading role in it for India captured the vision and imagination of the country's freedom fighters.

The following sections try to elaborate on this argument. Accordingly, the first section provides a brief account of the factors that determined the shaping of India's foreign policy during the Cold War period. The second section focuses on the drivers of 'Look East Policy'. The third section deals with the reasons behind the renaming of the LEP. The penultimate section deals with India's quest to emerge as a power of consequence in the multipolar world. The last section provides the concluding observations.

India's Nonalignment: Product of a Bipolar World

As noted already, the romantic impressions about the greatness of the age-old living civilisation influenced the shaping of independent India's foreign policy behaviour. Naturally, carving out a niche space for India among the league of the leading powers of the world became the fundamental precepts of the country's foreign policy. The civilisation legacy of India, its size, culture, history, geography and, above all, domestic and international political order influenced Nehru while crafting the non-aligned approach to India's foreign policy. The Hindu cultural ethos, Jainist, and Buddhist thought systems, formed the inner core of Nehru's vision on India's foreign and strategic policy, which received additional nourishment from the Islamic and Christian values and modern western rationality and the ethos of representative democracy. Gandhi's pacifist approach, rooted in the teachings of Gita, Jainism and Buddhism, had also influenced Nehru.

The plural and secular democratic approach to foreign and strategic policy maintained unstinting faith in democratic institutions and international organisations in conflict transformations. The core values of this stream of thought are strategic autonomy and faith in regional and international organisations' ability to mitigate conflicts. The *mandala* concept of concentric circles as codified by Kautilya in *Arthasastra* also influenced Nehruvian nonalignment and its inner core–the concept of strategic autonomy.

Notwithstanding the shift in emphasis at the operational level following the changes in the domestic and international milieu, the successive prime ministers of India followed the Nehruvian framework of nonalignment. It has to be underlined that nonalignment emphasised political and strategic autonomy along with a self-reliant growth path guided by the mixed economy policy framework without challenging the basic tenets of liberal capitalism, the international political economy of the post-war period. Nehru attempted to industrialise a dependent agrarian economy left behind by the retreating British colonialism with the support of borrowed technology and domestic capital. Since domestic capital was so fragile at that point of time, the Indian state had offered protection to the domestic capital from the possible onslaughts of international capital. At the same time, Nehru emphasised the importance of the creation of a robust public sector for economic growth and development of the country.

Nehru and Indira Gandhi very efficiently leveraged the flexibility of liberal capitalism and the bipolar division of international political order for promoting industrialisation of the country by import-substituting strategies and tactics. Indira Gandhi promoted the much-focused manner cooperation among the third world countries by promoting the group of 77 on the platform of New International Economic Order and South-South Cooperation. The leverage of equidistance internationally and mixed economy platform domestically for economic growth operated successfully within the overall framework of liberal capitalism–the dominant political economy platform of the period. According to a Chinese scholar during the Cold War period, 'India played a balancing act between the two superpowers, and created a somewhat significant influence on regional and international affairs, because of its leadership role in the nonalignment movement' (Zhao Hong, 2007, p. 127). Ashly Tellis (2016) had written that 'India's nonalignment aimed mainly at preventing U.S.-Soviet hostility from undermining its security, autonomy, and well-being at a time when the country was still relatively infirm'.

LEP: Imperative of a Unipolar Moment

The economic reforms initiated by the Narasimha Rao government just in the aftermath of the collapse of the bipolar world order led to massive readjustment in India's foreign, economic and strategic policy. When Narasimha Rao took over as Prime minister in June 1991, the country was reeling under the worst type of economic crisis since independence: "a steep fall in foreign exchange reserves to about US$ 1 billion (equal to two weeks' imports), a sharp downgrading of India's credit rating, and a cut-off of foreign private lending" (Joshy and Little, 1996, p. 14). Under the direction of IMF and World Bank, India introduced liberalisation, globalisation and privatisation policies with much enthusiasm. As a corollary, the Rao government initiated the 'Look East Policy' (LEP) with a noticeable strategic overtone to meet the demand for capital and to put the country on the track of economic growth by integrating Indian economy with the tiger economies of the East.

Since then, economics had emerged as the powerful locomotive of foreign policy calculus. Successive prime ministers took it forward. In a phased manner, the Narasimha Rao government and subsequently the Congress controlled United Progressive Alliance (UPA) coalitions I and II of Prime Minister Manmohan Singh as also the non-Congress governments that came to power during the UPA interregnum took forward policies promoting privatisation, liberalisation and globalisation of the economy. Acceptance of the international trade regime under the WTO umbrella, export-oriented industrialisation, FDI, and devaluing of the currency quite often fulfilled the conditions to get integrated into the new international economic architecture. These adjustments in the making of foreign policy were a result of the shift in international political economy from liberalism to neo-liberalism and in political terms, from a bipolar political order to the 'unipolar moment'.

The LEP, along with other policy measures, succeeded in rehabilitating the Indian economy with the international political economy of neo-liberalism. Also, LEP replaced the self-reliant economic strategy of Nehru-Indira period with comprehensive economic cooperation with East Asia in trade, services and investment. "The LEP signalled the end of India's previous pursuit of self-reliant economic development and the start of an era in which India strived to take advantage of new opportunities from international trade and investment. The LEP also emitted a strong signal that East Asia would be integral to India's economic opening. The region would no longer be overlooked, as it had been by India's previous foreign economic policy, but would now be regarded as a source of new business opportunity and inspiration for economic development" (AUSAID Working Paper, 2006).

Scholars have evaluated the LEP from both economic and strategic angles and found that results on the economic front were not that commendable (Basu and Ghosh, 2017); (De, U.K., 2014); (Lee, 2015); (Shivkumar and Delgado, 2011); (Naidu, 2004); (Palit, 2010); (Batabyal, 2006); (Muni, 2011); (Jenkins, 2003); (Mazumdar, 2011); (Sikri, 2009); (Ahmed, 2014); and (Basrur, 2017).

In merchandise trade with ASEAN, balance of trade is not favourable to India and ASEAN is not that willing to yield, as India wants trade in services where India enjoys a comparative advantage. However, when it comes to strategic relations, achievements are tangible. Partnership agreements with Japan, South Korea, Australia and bilateral agreements with certain of ASEAN members are instances of India's multiple engagements in East Asia during the LEP phase. It is noteworthy that the US took a pleasant and encouraging attitude towards India's engagements in the East. India responded positively by favourably inclining towards the rebalancing strategy of the US in the Asia-Pacific.

In short, the Look East pursued four objectives viz., reforms and liberalisation; sustained economic growth; regional economic integration and equity-based development (FIIA Briefing Paper 222, 2017). In other words, the 'Look East Policy' achieved its core objective of 'opening up export markets for India in absolute terms and ensuring that India is not left out of economic integration initiatives' (Lee, 2015).

Thus, initiation of LEP keeping the ASEAN as its fulcrum materialised its fundamental objective of getting integrated to the political economy of neo-liberal globalisation. It has also brought-in strategic dividend for India by becoming closer to the US strategy in the Asia-Pacific. India just remained one step short of becoming part of the Hub and Spoke alliance system in Asia promoted by the US in the Asia-Pacific (Lee, 2015). India instead favoured a strategy of multi-alignment and strategic partnership with like-minded global and regional states.

AEP: Strategic Interconnect in a Multi-polar World

In 2014, when Modi took over the reins of the country with a massive mandate, several observers of India's foreign policy expected that there would be a complete break from the policies (Chellaney, 2014; Mohan, 2015) pursued by the previous Congress and Congress party-controlled coalition governments in New Delhi. However, many analysts subsequently noted an essential continuity in Modi's foreign policy (Hall, 2015; Basrur, 2017). The kind of muscularity that was expected by many was not found. Instead Modi pursued a policy of astute pragmatism as is evident from the strategies of networking with significant powers of the world including United States, Russia, Japan France, South Korea and to a lesser extent with China for capacity building initiatives, status-seeking for upward mobility with a tinge of strategic restraint and conscious pursuance of dependence avoidance (Basrur, 2017). Thus, any evaluation of 'Act East Policy' has to keep in mind the astute pragmatism as noted above.

While answering a question in the parliament, the Minister of State for External Affairs of India stated that AEP 'focuses on the extended neighbourhood in the Asia-Pacific region' (Ministry of External Affairs, 2011) primarily with economic objectives which subsequently got extended to political and cultural domains.

The Minister further elaborated that AEP's objective has been to promote economic cooperation with the East Asian countries for India's domestic development including infrastructure development, manufacturing, trade, skills, urban renewal, smart cities, Make in India, connectivity projects, Digital India cooperation in space, science and technology, tourism promotion, people-to-people contact etc. Another priority area of AEP is the development of North-Eastern states India in general and Arunachal Pradesh in particular. Institutional mechanisms at a bilateral, regional and multilateral level got established to promote connectivity and commerce. 'Connectivity of North-East with the ASEAN region through trade, culture, people-to-people contacts and physical infrastructure (road, airport, telecommunication and power) has been emphasised as a priority area of AEP.

The Kaladan Multi-modal Transit Transport Project, the India-Myanmar-Thailand Trilateral Highway Project, Rhi-Tiddim Road Project and Border Haats are some of the significant projects undertaken. In August 2015, the ASEAN-India Plan of Action for the period 2016-20 had been adopted which identified areas of cooperation and stepped up activities to enhance partnership with regional and Multilateral organisation such as ASEAN, ARF, EAS, BIMSTEC, ACD, MCG and IORA.

On the cultural side, Buddhist and Hindu links got energised to develop new contacts and connectivity between people. Measures, including building transport infrastructure, encouraging airlines to enhance connectivity in the region, and contacts between academic and cultural institutions are also envisaged. The Minister further elaborated that the ASEAN-India Agreement on Trade in Service and Investments had entered into force for India and seven ASEAN countries from July 1, 2015. The ASEAN-India Trade Negotiating Committee has been tasked to undertake a review of the ASEAN-India Trade in Goods Agreement. India had also invited ASEAN member states to participate in the International Solar Alliance which it has co-launched with France on November 30, 2015, at COP-21.

On strategic issues, we have increasing convergence on security interests with key partners both in a bilateral and multilateral format. Closer cooperation in combating terrorism, collaborating for peace and stability in the region and promotion of maritime security based on international norms and laws are being pursued. India has elevated those relations to a strategic partnership with Indonesia, Vietnam, Malaysia, Japan, Republic of Korea (ROK), Australia, Singapore and the Association of Southeast Asian Nations (ASEAN) and evolved friendly ties with all nations in the Asia-Pacific region. Apart from ASEAN, ASEAN Regional Forum (ARF) and East Asia Summit (EAS), India has been actively engaging in regional fora such as Bay of Bengal Initiative for Multi-Sectoral Technical and Economic Cooperation (BIMSTEC), Asia Cooperation Dialogue (ACD), Mekong-Ganga Cooperation (MGC) and the Indian Ocean Rim Association (IORA).

Thus, the geographic coverage of AEP got extended to Japan, Australia, Pacific Islands, South Korea and Mongolia. Of these engagements, the relationship with Japan attained the status of the most dynamic one. Signing of civilian nuclear deal, high-speed railway project, cooperation on the Delhi-Mumbai industrial corridor, defence cooperation with partnership in Malabar exercises are some of the achievements of Modi's AEP.

While addressing the Heads of Indian Mission from across the world, Modi has stated that the present global environment represents a rare opportunity when the world is keen to embrace India, and India is moving forward with confidence. He urged them to use this unique opportunity to help India position itself in a leading role, rather than just a balancing force, regionally. Urging the mission heads to shed old mindsets, the Prime Minister exhorted them to adapt themselves to changing global situations.

From the above, it is apparent that Modi has grasped the shift properly in international political order from that of the 'unipolar moment' to multi-polarity. Modi's ambition is to make India one of the strong pillars of the emerging multipolar international system.

It seems that Prime Minister Modi's 'Act East Policy' manifests a departure from the strategy of creating a sphere of influence in its immediate neighbourhood, based on the concentric circle formula of the nonalignment era. India's eastward focus attempts to establish a strategic partnership with significant powers in the East for security and economic cooperation.

The economic pronouncements of Prime Minister Modi indicated that he would continue, on a fast pace, with the reforms that were initiated in 1991 by Prime Minister Narasimha Rao and pursued by his immediate predecessors Manmohan Singh and Vajpayee. We can notice in Narendra Modi's approach of 'strategic interconnectedness' or 'multi-vectored engagement', a continuity that goes perfectly in agreement with the policies of his immediate predecessors. According to Rajiv Bhatia, AEP is a newer version of the LEP with five additional features. Firstly, the focus is on tangible action and concrete results. Secondly, keeping ASEAN as the central pillar or core of the policy, South Bloc extended and deepened cooperation with US, Japan, Australia and South Korea to act as a counterweight to the ever-increasing influence of China in the Indian Ocean.

Consequently, the policy added some boldness on India's part in the domains of security and defence strategy. Fourthly, India became more cordial and cooperative with the ASEAN. Finally, the North-East of India received a higher priority in the overall scheme of AEP (Bhatia, 2018). In the view of Muley, the goals of 'Act East Policy' are two-pronged: 'boost India's standing as a regional power by initiating increased cooperation in the region and act as a counterweight to the increasing strategic influence of China' (Muley, 2017). However, foreign policy behaviour of Modi has amply demonstrated that the aims, objectives and strategic outlook of the policy pursued by him are intended not just to boost India's regional status but to emerge as a global player with confidence on the strength of its growing economy, strategic hedging and partnerships.

There exists a symbiotic relationship between foreign policy strategy and domestic economic growth. It seems that Modi's Make in India project tried to draw its nourishment from finance capital, and the politico-strategic doctrine got constructed on the plank of multi-vectored alignment or strategic interconnectedness.

The clear message is that Modi wanted to look beyond the canons of nonalignment with the pragmatism of unprecedented nature. India is now part of organisations of diverse nature such as G-20, East Asia Summit, BRICS, and Shanghai Cooperation Organisation. Of late, India has shown a renewed interest in the Commonwealth which it had ignored all along these years.

Modi's continuous interactions in the last five years with the leaders from the neighbourhood, the Japanese Prime minister, the Chinese President and, above all, with the former US President Barack Obama and later with President Donald Trump, has demonstrated Modi's pragmatism. It is worth mentioning here that immediately after inking the partnership agreement with the US President Obama, Prime Minister Modi asked his external affairs Minister to prepare the ground for his visit to China in May 2015.

Similarly, immediately after concluding the QUAD meeting, India hosted in Delhi the trilateral summit meeting of India, China and Russia. The above-said policy signified what could be called hedging strategy: "hedging is a term derived from economic theory whereby actors invest in different policies to ensure against failures. Hedging includes external security cooperation with third countries through the formation of so-called partnerships but, importantly, also entails integration and cooperation mechanisms with the country that forms the object of future uncertainty. In other words, hedging combines balancing as well as engagement strategies" (Gaens and Ruohomaki, 2017).

The post-Cold War international power structure is symptomatic of the overarching politico-military dominance of the US, which acts as a protective shield of the international political economy managed by the Wall Street-WTO-World Bank complex. However, scholarly assessment is that the politico-military dominance of the US is on the decline, and multiple power centres are being shaped in different parts of the world. However, on several counts, the US rebalancing strategy in the Indo-Pacific region finds strategic convergence with India's LEP/AEP. More than an external economic policy or a political slogan, the LEP/AEP is a strategic shift in India's vision of the world and its place in the evolving global political economy.

It is also a manifestation of India's belief that developments in East Asia are of direct consequence to its security and development. Therefore, India has been nurturing the bond of friendship and cooperation with East Asia; and that has a strong economic foundation and a cooperative paradigm of positive inter-connectedness of security interests. The AEP, the refurbished version of LEP, represents a reorientation of India's foreign economic policy with strategic overtones in the aftermath of the demise of the Soviet Union.

Also, it is worth mentioning here that India is a part of multilateral interaction with its membership in the five-nation grouping called BRICS (Brazil, Russia, India, China and South Africa) to strengthen mutual relationships. This grouping's political interaction could help to alter the shape of the international financial system and the global economy. One of the objectives of the grouping is the democratisation of international financial institutions. The joint declaration at the first summit meeting held in Russia focused on global food security. The BRICS countries supported the adoption of a wide range of mid- to long-term measures to provide for a solution to the issue of food security.

Similarly, RCEP negotiations are progressing very fast. We can only hope at this moment that India's interest in accommodating the service sector in the ambit of RCEP would be well taken. Hope every member nations' interest would get space in a mutually acceptable manner (Haider, 2019).

Concluding Observations

In 2014, when Modi came to power, everyone expected a muscular foreign policy, a distinct departure from the policies of Congress regimes, right from Nehru. However, the foreign policy behaviour of Prime Minister Narendra Modi with his Sangh Parivar background did not demonstrate such a clear departure from the Nehruvian framework of foreign policy making. Modi's vision and mission are entirely in agreement with Nehruvian aspirations to make India visible in the world as a nation of consequence. We have already noted that the Nehruvian framework of nonalignment did not attempt to delink from the liberal capitalist world order.

Instead, the flexibility that was embedded in liberal capitalism was leveraged by the Congress of Nehru and Indira Gandhi to fulfil the objective of import substitution industrialisation–the dominant paradigm of economic growth and development during that period. Since the social structure of accumulation in contemporary capitalism of monopolies is different from that of 'embedded liberalism' (Harvey, 2005), such leverage was hardly available for the post-reform governments in India; and LEP initiated India's integration with the neo-liberal world order. Narasimha Rao managed the switch over to the LPG with ease at the historical juncture of 'unipolar moment'.

Governments of Vajpayee and Manmohan Singh could not tune the Indian economy fully following the requirements of reigning international economic architecture because of weakness imposed by the political coalition and the stiff resistance offered by certain social formations in general and the left political parties in particular. Even then both of them promoted free-market economy to the extent possible. Modi sensed the gradual decline of the 'unipolar' moment and the emergence of multipolar world order. China's assertive presence in and around South Asia is also visible on the radar of Modi's establishment.

Modi shaped AEP and other multiple engagements and partnerships based on a proper grasp of the emerging multipolar world order with a massive presence of China in it. The polymerous engagement under the AEP and the hedging strategy to moderate China has been the major shift in India's foreign policy.

From the above, we could glean that the craving for a space in the big league of nations, the quintessence of nonalignment, is a reasonably constant element in the foreign policy strategy of India. This craving for recognition as a leading power is, in fact, a civilizational legacy, very well ingrained in the collective psyche of Indians. Therefore, the natural course of action is that India has to adjust and remodel its politico-strategic calculations following the shifts in the international architecture of politics and economics. Such an adjustment or remodelling started unfolding with the initiation of the LPG reforms in India.

However, weak central governments crippled by the coalition's pressures could not facilitate the expansion of neo-liberal globalisation in India as envisaged. In the 2014 general elections, we witnessed the collapse of the Congress system and the ultimate victory for the Hindu nationalist BJP under the strong leadership of Narendra Modi. This victory has given Modi to take necessary policy initiatives at the domestic and international front to integrate Indian economy fully with that of the global economy and to play the game of divergence and convergence with China in the multi-polar international system.

The most crucial aspect of India's aspirations to become a leading power is that India plays the game in the lap of the political economy of capitalism despite the rhetoric of socialism during the Nehru-Indira period. Thus, the natural course of action is that India adjusted and remodelled its politico-strategic calculations following the shifts in the international political economy. Such an adjustment or remodelling started unfolding with the initiation of the LPG reforms in India.

However, weak central governments crippled by coalition's pressures could not facilitate the expansion of neo-liberal globalisation in India as envisaged. In the 2014 general elections, we witnessed the collapse of the Congress system and the ultimate victory for the Hindu nationalist BJP under the strong leadership of Prime Minister Narendra Modi. BJP's Hindu nationalism in alliance with the business class in trade and commerce-enabled Modi to accelerate economic neo-liberalism further as is evident from policies like demonetisation and GST internally and full integration with the international economic architecture externally.

References

Ahmed, W. (2014), "The Political Economy and Geopolitical Context of India's Economic Crisis,1990-91", *Singapore Journal of Tropical Geography,* 35, 179-195.

Bajpai, K. (2017), "Narendra Modi's Pakistan and China Policy: Assertive Bilateral Diplomacy, Active Coalition Diplomacy", *International Affairs,* 93(1), 69-91.

Basrur, R. (2017), "Modi's Foreign Policy Fundamentals: A Trajectory Unchanged", *International Affairs*, 93(1), 7-26.

Basu, S. and Ghosh, S. (2017), FDI in India: Understanding the Implications for Growth and Job Creation", *Journal of Management and Public Policy*, 9(1), 5-16.

Business Line (2017, November 11), "PM to Attend India-ASEAN, East Asia Summits", *Business Line,* Chennai: The Hindu.

Chachavalpongpun, P. (2011), "Look East Meets Look West: Indian-Southeast Asian Relations in Flux", *The International Spectator*, 46(2), 91-108.

Chacko, P. (2015), "The New Geo-Economic of a 'Rising' India: The State of Transformation and the Recasting of Foreign Policy", *Journal of Contemporary Asia*, 45(2), 326-344.

Chatterjee, S. (2007), "Conceptions of Space in India's Look East Policy: Order, Cooperation or Community?", *South Asian Survey*, 14(1), 65-81.

De, U.K. (2014), "India's Look East for Integration with East Asia: Step Towards Progress", *Journal of International Economics*, 6(1), 105-21.

Economic and Political Weekly Editorial (2010), "India's Look East Policy", *Economic and Political Weekly*, XLV(48), 8.

Haokip, T. (2011), "India's Look East Policy: Prospects and Challenges for Northeast India", in Z. Hussain, 'India's Look

East Policy and North-East India: Achievements and Constraints', pp. 1-7, New Delhi.

Hong, Z. (2007), "India and China: Rivals or Partners in South Asia?", *Contemporary Southeast Asia*, 29(1), 121-142.

Jagran.com (2011, November 23), available at: www.firstpost.com/world/us-supports-india-llok-east-policy-137741.

Jenkins, R. (2003), "India's States and the Making of Foreign Economic Policy: The Limits of the Constituent Diplomacy Paradigm", *The Journal of Federalism*, 33(4), 63-81.

John, D. (2014), "How Prospects for Global Economic Growth Influence India's Foreign Policy", *Strategy and Leadership*, 42(2), 1-5.

Karmarker, S. (2005), "India-ASEAN Cooperation in Services", Indian Council for Research on International Economic Relations, New Delhi.

Kugelman, M. (2013), "India's Foreign Policy Fog", *Current Wilson Quarterly* (Autumn), 20-22.

Lee, L. (2015), "India as Nation of Consequence in Asia: The Potential and Limitations of India's Act East Policy", *The Journal of East Asian Affairs*, 29(2), 67-104.

Lombard, M. and Lombard, A. (2011), "A Comparative Analysis of Effects of Foreign Direct Investment in China's and India's Economic Development in Recent Years", *Economic Papers*, 10(4), 522-529.

Mazumdar, A. (2011), "India's Search for a Post-Cold War Foreign Policy", *India Quarterly*, 67(2), 165-182.

Ministry of External Affairs (2011, November 23), "India-ASEAN Relations", New Delhi.

Muni, S.D. (2011), "India's Look East Policy: The Strategic Dimensions", *ISAS Working Paper*, 1-25, Singapore: National University of Singapore.

Muni, S.D. (2012), "Obama Administration's Pivot to Asia-Pacific and India's Role", ISAS Working Paper, Singapore: National University of Singapore.

Palit, A. (2010), "India's 'Look East' Policy: Reflecting the Future", The National University of Singapore, Institute of South Asian Studies: Singapore.

Shivkumar, V. and Delgado, J.E. (2011), 'Look East Policy' of India: The Myths and Realities", *Tercera Epoca*, 5(10), 107-132.

Sikri, R. (2009), "India's 'Look East' Policy", *Asia Pacific Review*, Vol. 16(1), 131-145.

Zhang, D. (2006), "India Looks East: Strategies and Impacts", AusAID Public Affairs Group, Canberra.

2

India-ASEAN Institutional Partnership in Maritime Security

S. Utham Kumar Jamadhagni

As India celebrates her 25 years of enduring ties with ASEAN it is pertinent to examine in depth, the field of maritime security at this juncture and the future areas that would need focus and attention. With the geographical reality of being island nations or heavily dependent on sea lanes for trade, maritime security is highly significant for this successful Southeast Asian association. India as a huge peninsular country also derives immensely from its coastal orientation. Thus, it is imperative that the two bring more attention to this aspect of the relations.

The existing interactive mechanisms be it ASEAN-India Summit, ARF, ASEAN Defence Ministers Meeting+ (ADMM+) and the recent ASEAN-India Commemorative Summit, have all served as fora for discussions on maritime security specifics. However, much progress on the physical accessibility to ASEAN countries through the maritime routes has been rather slow. Projects that propose greater connectivity could augur mutual benefits. The incumbent government's fillip to deepen ties with ASEAN through the "Act East Policy", offers ample scope to develop the agenda further. Ambitious national development plans along the lines of Sagarmala retrain India's attention to the maritime realm. In all these, the contribution of ASEAN countries and chance for mutual cooperation need to be fully comprehended with and given a boost.

The paper thus aims to highlight the imminent need for placing special emphasis on maritime security in India-ASEAN relations. It also examines the role maritime security could play as a galvaniser in stronger institutionalisation of this significant linkage. It not only reviews the advantage that has been garnered in this field in the past but more importantly the future possibilities it holds for congruity of interests for India and ASEAN. The paper would also attempt to suggest areas that might improve maritime security for both the entities.

Action on Act East

India as an emergent power aims to build new ties and nurture old friendships especially in the greater Asian region. ASEAN serves as the lynchpin of India's 'Act East Policy'. As India gains a closer look at neighbouring countries and regions, the ASEAN-India connect is under renewed focus. Not only is the global economic interdependence warranting deeper ties but strategic and cultural imperatives also present additional dimensions to such interaction. The first ever presence of heads of state of all 10 members of the ASEAN at the 69th Indian Republic Day official celebration symbolises the importance India attaches to the growing ties with this important region. It can be seen as a "dramatic declaration of intent by New Delhi to boost India's ties with Southeast Asia". [1]

ASEAN is geographically proximate to India sharing land borders with Burma, and sea borders with Thailand, Indonesia, Malaysia and Singapore. India-ASEAN relations have deepened and intensified significantly in recent years. The 'Look East Policy' took the cultural, geographical connects into account and the potential role the Diaspora could play in bridging the gaps between India and their host countries. This policy sought to foster closer links with ASEAN in strategic, political and economic fields. In the words of Prime Minister Dr. Manmohan Singh, "India's Look East Policy is not merely an external economic policy, it is also a strategic shift in India's vision of the world and India's place in the evolving global economy. Most of all, it is about reaching out to our civilisational neighbours in Southeast Asia and East Asia". The relationship moved to a higher level of depth and focus with the unveiling of the "Act East" policy.

Progress Report

Continued and sustained engagement at the individual state level as well as the regional level has been adopted by India. Economic interaction has grown manifold and the scope for increase in trade ties has widened to other areas. Since India has no issues with any of the ASEAN countries, the ground for stronger ties has already been laid. The emphasis on infrastructure development as a means of enhancing physical connectivity with the ASEAN has been exhibited with the proposed projects like India-Myanmar-Thailand Trilateral Highway and the Kaladan Multi-Modal Transit Transport Project. Other areas have also been identified. However, it is now imminent to review the movement made in the proposed plans and projects in order to gain an understanding of the tasks that need immediate attention as well as lacunas that have to be addressed in execution and implementation.

The above mentioned ongoing joint infrastructure projects have been progressing slowly. The Kaladan project aims to connect India's eastern seaport of Kolkata with Sittwe seaport in Myanmar by sea; it will then link Sittwe seaport to Lashio in Myanmar via Kaladan river boat route and then from Lashio on to Mizoram by road transport. The Sittwe port is being developed by India.

The Friendship highway that links Moreh in Manipur, India to Bangkok, Thailand through Myanmar is awaiting completion by 2020. It is also proposed to be extended to other ASEAN countries of Laos, Cambodia and Vietnam.

The DRDO projects seeking international cooperation have been in the pipeline for long. The sale of anti-tank missiles to Southeast Asian countries by India has not fructified. A previous arms supply of 100 submachine guns and 50 sniper rifles to Vietnam fell through, enabling Pakistan to complete the sale. Line of credit given to Vietnam for the purchase of four off shore patrol vessels has been completed after much delay. Retracing of ancient maritime routes and cultural connect under *Project Mausam* is yet to take off. The Project aims to understand how monsoons shaped interaction across Indian Ocean leading to "spread of shared knowledge systems, traditions, technologies and ideas along maritime routes". [2] The setting up of a White Shipping Data Fusion centre has also not seen the light of the day. The proposal was made by the then Vice President of India Hamid Ansari at the first summit of IORA in Jakarta in 2017. [3] There was also a suggestion to set up an IORA Centre of Excellence to provide academics and researchers access to a collective source of data and resource material. [4]

The Regional Comprehensive Economic Partnership is another plan that is awaiting India's approval. India's early resolution of issues related to the conclusion of a Regional Comprehensive Economic Partnership with the ASEAN would go a long way in boosting confidence. India is concerned about the unfettered access to Chinese goods while there is lack of access to Indian services sector. [5]

India-ASEAN Summit

The commemorative Summit for 25 years of India ASEAN relations was held in January 2018. The Delhi Declaration signed during this summit reaffirms India's commitment in nurturing ties with the region in a mutually beneficial manner. It includes special mention of maritime security as an area of immense import. Specifically, the declaration talks of the employment of the Expanded ASEAN Maritime Forum (EAMF) to "address common challenges on maritime issues". [6] The EAMF is a track 1.5 diplomatic initiative focusing on cross-cutting maritime issues of common concern.

India also assured that it would cooperate with ASEAN "to enhance collaboration in the maritime domain". [7] Prime Minister Modi in his address referred to the aspects of humanitarian and disaster relief, security cooperation and freedom of navigation as key focus areas of maritime cooperation. [8] There was a suggestion even for an ASEAN-India women navy team circumnavigating the world. An India-ASEAN Maritime Transportation Agreement is on the cards. India believes that there is requirement for "urgent modernisation in the context of current geopolitical realities" [9] of maritime connectivity.

This aims to eliminate barriers hindering maritime transport and seeks to establish regional maritime transport network as a response to China's Belt and Road Initiative. This Agreement would help improve access to maritime services through greater transparency in maritime regulations, policies and practices of trading partners; facilitating the flow of commercial goods at sea and ports; and paving the way for establishment of joint ventures in the fields of maritime transportation, shipbuilding and repairs, maritime training, information technology including development of simulators, port facilities and related maritime activities.

Soon a taskforce on maritime connectivity will be constituted to look into a coastal shipping network, develop maritime cargo routes between Indian and ASEAN and establish a coastal shipping service as well as suggest training and capacity building programs.

ADMM+

The ASEAN Defence Ministers'+ meeting with ASEAN countries plus the US, China, Russia, Japan, India, South Korea, Australia and New Zealand principally seeks to discuss non-traditional security agenda. Being a member of this group, India's role has to be more active. A recent extension to the plan of action for years 2010-2015 for the ASEAN-India Partnership for Peace, Progress and Shared Prosperity looks at promoting the ADMM+ as "a useful platform for dialogue and security cooperation, in particular for forging practical cooperation to address the security challenges facing the region". This document also specifically mentions maritime safety and search and rescue by mutual sharing of experience, cooperation in technological areas and exchange visits of concerned authorities.

Hosting of ADMM+ summit in the future by India would exhibit her commitment. While Australia and New Zealand are organising the summits regularly, India is yet to host even one. Humanitarian mine action is the only area India is offering expertise under the aegis of ADMM+.

The first ASEAN India Workshop on the Blue Economy was held in Hanoi jointly by India and Vietnam in December 2017. It aimed to identify opportunities and challenges in developing the Blue Economy; build necessary institutional frameworks to support regional countries in developing the Blue Economy; foster support and commitments from regional countries and intergovernmental organizations in advancing the Blue Economy; and seek to integrate a Blue Economy approach into national and regional development strategies, making it a regional cooperation priority area.

Near Neighbours

On the bilateral level, India has been engaging with each of the ASEAN members and promoting several aspects of maritime security and related fields.

Myanmar as the contiguous neighbour evokes special concern and is interested in her economic rebuilding. The South Indian Textile Restoration Association is being tasked with the revival of Burmese textile units. India has favoured Quick Impact Projects in Cambodia and offered ₹ 500 crore as project development fund including a centre for IT excellence. The number of such projects has also been increased for Cambodia from 5 to 10. [10] The Archaeological Survey of India has been extensively involved in the restoration of the temples at Angor Wat and Ta Prohm earlier. Currently, India seeks to undertake conservation of the ancient Shiva temple at Preah Vihar. India is offering Laos an e-data gathering, invoicing and collection software called SkyRev 360. Promoting private partnership in port development, the Indian firm Adani Ports will jointly develop an integrated maritime city in Carey Island as well as the expansion of Port Klang, the 12th largest port in the world.

Closest Ally

Vietnam has been one of the special friends of India in the ASEAN group. The deepening ties with this small Southeast Asian country should also be weighed against the rising influence of the other Asian giant China, in the region. In the area of maritime security, India insists on freedom of navigation in the South China Sea with respect for international legal provisions. Energy security is another focus area in India-Vietnam relations. India also figures as an important defence supplier to this country. There have been recent reports of India's sale of the supersonic Brahmos missile to Vietnam, though the same has not been confirmed by Indian sources.

Interestingly, during the Doklam issue, no official statement was issued by the Vietnamese government. On the other hand, India is also seen as a "fence sitter" [11] still holding on to its Cold War era, non-aligned policy. According to Cmde Ashok Rai in his *Naval War Journal* article remarks, that India's actions could "send confusing signals" about her professed role as net provider and reliability in times of crises to countries looking for her to assume a regional leadership role. [12]

Staunch Support

As a nation that has always been a strong advocate of India in the ASEAN forum, Singapore holds a special place among the group members. From being a sectoral partner in 1992 to a full dialogue partner in 1995 and then inclusion in the East Asia Summit in 2005, India has received complete support from Singapore. Singapore is ready to advance its investment opportunities for India as well as scope for new ones like ASEAN Smart Cities Network. [13] In fact, Singapore will be developing India's first Smart City, Amaravati, Andhra Pradesh's capital. [14]

Indonesia and India's trade potential could reach US$ 2.1 billion with agreements signed as a result of the Indonesia India Business Forum meet on January 22, 2018. [15] Recently, India and Philippines signed an investment facilitation agreement. [16]

Unfinished Tasks

A cultural project called "Sailing to Swarnabhumi" aims to map India's maritime encounters with the Southeast Asian nations and the impact on the cultures of the two entities. Next documentation of inscriptions of Indian nobles, traders and others along the Mekong River is also being proposed.

Other Power Interest

Added to the woes of India's non-adherence to deadlines and delays in project delivery is the heightened interest the other powers have shown in the region. This includes China which has huge stakes in the ASEAN region. It has been offering financial help to many countries and delivering on promises of infrastructure development and other facilities. China has initiated a deep sea port project in Myanmar at Kyaukpyu. The Asian Highway is another infrastructure project that is being implemented with full vigour.

Philippines received 3,000 assault rifles from China last year after US earlier stopped a sale of 26,000 M4 rifles. Thailand received 28 V4 MBTs from China at the cost of US$ 147 million. Type 039A Yuan-class diesel-electric attack submarines will also be delivered shortly. [17]

Four Chinese coastal patrol vessels worth US$ 227 million are bound for Malaysia. [18] Chinese companies are also extensively investing in port expansion plans in Malaysia including Melaka Gateway, Kuala Linggi Port, Penang Port and the Kuantan port projects. With Burma, China enjoys a special relationship. It is the largest supplier of arms and includes a variety of equipment like fighter aircrafts, armoured vehicles, guns and naval ships. [19]

China transferred two frigates of Type 053H1. Indonesia would purchase C-802 anti-ship missiles, portable surface-to-air missiles and air search radars as well as Type 730 ship Bourne close-in weapon system. In Indonesia, China has taken up the Kalibaru project that seeks to expand the nation's largest port, Tanjung Priok. [20]

China has increased manifold her economic investment in the ASEAN region and it is now at a whopping six times higher than the Indian investments. [21] Though ASEAN is now India's 4th largest trading partner at US$ 71 billion making up around 10 percent of India's total external trade, it is relatively small compared to Chinese trading volumes. [22] China's trade with ASEAN is slated to reach the US$ 1 trillion by 2020. [23]

USA is another country with interest in ASEAN. She has provided fast attack crafts to the countries of ASEAN and is in the process of implementing the Southeast Asia Maritime Security Initiative aimed at offering help in training personnel, offering military equipment and building defence hardware in the region.

Conclusion

India is seeking to expand its footprint on the world strategic map, and hence widening the scope of relations with significant regions of the world like Southeast Asia is mandatory. This is reflected in the maritime area too. Ever since becoming a full-dialogue partner of ASEAN in 1995, India has gradually increased the manner of maritime engagement. While it might be strong at the individual bilateral level, that with ASEAN is yet to reach full fruition.

India has continued to engage the Southeast Asian region in the maritime realm. The tailor-made naval exercises like the coordinated patrol exercises with Indonesia, or the deep ties nurtured with the constant friend Singapore signify the range of activities India has been engaging in. The periodic conduct of exercises in the South China Sea considered an area of possible future conflict can be seen as a test of India's power projection capabilities. There are also new initiatives with countries like Burma. India's humanitarian assistance through its naval assets especially during the tsunami and such other natural calamities has also cemented ties.

The India-ASEAN Summit and the ADMM+ are steps in the right direction in creating greater scope for widening nature of engagement in areas including the maritime sector. Being an adjacent region with no apparent conflict over maritime boundaries and convergence of interests in maintenance of maritime security, ASEAN offers immense opportunities at strengthening relationship.

Maintaining safety of sea lanes including the prevention or at least control of maritime terrorism as well as keenly watching China's engagement with the ASEAN region means that India should enhance cooperation in the vital field of maritime security. The Narendra Modi government's 'Act East Policy' exhibits this intent amply and must build on the hopes and aspirations it has announced and should strive to achieve the same.

The shared interest in preserving the major sea lanes from the Indian Ocean to the Pacific also brings ASEAN and India closer. [24] In his opening remarks for the ASEAN-India Commemorative Summit Plenary in New Delhi, India, on January 25, 2018, Singaporean PM Hsien Loong highlighted the importance of expanding air, land, maritime, and digital connectivity between India and ASEAN as it "will reinforce business and people-to-people links between both sides and benefit both our peoples". [25] India has announced a US$ 1 billion line of credit to fulfil the physical and digital connectivity as per the Master Plan on ASEAN Connectivity 2025 and

ASEAN ICT Masterplan 2020. [26] Development of India-ASEAN maritime framework using Bay of Bengal as an "exploratory ground" could be one of the areas that need attention.

However, care must be taken to address the operationalisation delays that affect the proposed plans and projects. As indicated by *The Hindu* in one of its editorials, "it must not be forgotten that when ASEAN-India leaders last gathered in New Delhi in 2012 to mark the 20th anniversary of the Dialogue Partnership, they had made a similar commitment to trade and maritime security and several promises were "yet to be realised". [27] Promises must be converted to deliverables. The timely completion of projects even if module and phase-wise instead of multilateral ambitions that are bogged down by clearances or delays, must definitely be adopted. This would encourage more of the ASEAN countries to seek Indian assistance in the maritime infrastructure related areas.

It goes on to conclude that heavy lifting is required to integrate India into the ASEAN equation or else shared history and culture and political leadership in sync may only yield rousing summitry.

Expanding areas to non-navy and coast guard is imperative because though we have robust naval exercises and other activities, maritime data sharing could be a vital area.

Under the aegis of Expanded ASEAN Maritime Framework, USA has suggested sea farers training and education for civilian maritime personnel. Such initiatives can be invited. India has also established the East Asia Summit Virtual Knowledge Portal on Disaster Management. [28]

Eco-tourism and best practises in managing marine resources and protecting them could be another way forward. With the 2019 year being declared a tourism year by both the entities, promotion of eco-tourism could be an attractive alternative. The impact of effective best practices in achieving sustainability as well as deriving benefits from management of marine resources could be discussed at the regional level together with bilateral efforts. The contribution of the Blue Economy to both India and ASEAN could be further enhanced by collaborative research and adoption of successful local attempts from either side.

Financing the many projects is also an issue. India does not adopt a financing like the Chinese so either we have to offer line of credit or completely bear the expense towards the projects. The widespread dissemination of information regarding projects that have been successfully completed by India is also the need of the hour. The completion of the Chabahar port and handing over to the Iranians was a low key affair instead of being showcased as a triumphant strategic and economic move.

The hopes and aspirations of ASEAN countries as a whole in India playing a significant role in forging deeper and more meaningful ties must be acknowledged and recognised. India must also look for new areas of maritime cooperation that would derive mutual benefit from closer interaction with India's maritime neighbour. Reassessment of existing and ongoing projects for addressing the possible lacuna in implementation especially timely delivery would go a long way in enhancing confidence in India's stated objectives for the relations. Instead of establishing new mechanisms, existing institutional arrangements like the ADMM+, East Asia Summit and others could be used effectively to enlist greater cooperation in areas that have already been identified.

Maritime cooperation is one of the most promising fields that can foster increased interaction as it not only has ancient linkages in the form of maritime routes but modern imperatives also that could garner economic and social benefits for India and ASEAN alike. Added to this is the reality of heightened concern for maritime security that includes ensuring freedom of navigation in the seas surrounding the two geographical contiguities, protecting sea lanes of communication and preserving the resources of marine origin that principally support development of individual countries.

Multi-sectoral focus for enhancing interaction together with earnest efforts at addressing issues related to existing and prospective plans for improvement needs to be taken up. India's envisaged role as "net security provider" should be illustrated through timely and concerted assistance to ASEAN members in crisis situations.

Unless India is prepared to play the role of a balancer in the Asian strategic calculus augmenting its influence in the region while simultaneously willing to circumscribe it along the wishes of the ASEAN countries, the future prospects of deepening relationship with this significant world region would only remain an unfulfilled promise.

Endnotes

1. Harsh Pant (2018), "The Arc of Southeast Asia", *The Hindu,* January 25.
2. http://www.indiaculture.nic.in/project-mausam.
3. "India Offers to Host Information Centre for Maritime Security", *The Economic Times*, March 7, 2017, available at: https://economictimes.indiatimes.com/news/defence/india-offers-to-host-information-centre-for-maritime-security/articleshow/57518034.cms.
4. Ibid.
5. "New Delhi Brims with Look East Vibes", *The Hindu*, January 25, 2018.
6. Delhi Declaration of the ASEAN-India Commemorative Summit to mark the 25th Anniversary of ASEAN-India Dialogue Relations , PIB, Government of India, January 25, 2018.
7. *The Indian Express*, January 25, 2018, available at: http://indianexpress.com/article/india/freedom-of-navigation-will-be-key-focus-of-india-asean-in-the-maritime-domain-pm-narendra-modi-5039235.
8. "ASEAN-India Summit: PM Modi Harks Back to Shared Voyage between India and SE Asia", *The Strait Times,* January 25, 2018, available at:

http://www.straitstimes.com/asia/south-asia/asean-india-summit-pm-modi-harks-back-to-shared-voyage-between-india-and-se-asia.

9. "India, ASEAN Leaders Agree to Boost Maritime Cooperation", *The Economic Times,* January 26, 2018.
10. "India, Cambodia Sign Four Agreements", *The Pioneer*, February 5, 2018.
11. Cmde Ashok Rai (2017), "Is India's Vietnam Quid Pro Quo for China's Pakistan?", *Naval War College Journal*, Vol. 29, Annual Issue, pp. 111-120.
12. Ibid.
13. "Facilitating Business Opportunities with Smart Cities Network", *The Strait Times*, February 2, 2018, available at: http://www.straitstimes.com/singapore/facilitating-business-opportunities-with-smart-cities-network.
14. "Amaravati Masterplan AP to Ink MoU with Singapore Government Today", *The Hindu Business Line*, May 13, 2017, available at: https://www.thehindubusinessline.com/news/national/amaravati-masterplan-ap-to-ink-mou-with-singapore-govt-today/article9697352.ece.
15. "Indonesia, India Trade Agreements Reach US$ 2.1 Billion", *Republika.co.id*, January 26, 2018, available at: http://en.republika.co.id/berita/en/national-politics/18/01/26/p35v7e414-indonesia-india-trade-agreements-reach-us21-billion.
16. "India, Philippines Sign Investment Facilitation Agreement", *The Indian Express*, January 25, 2018, available at: http://www.newindianexpress.com/nation/2018/jan/25/india-philippines-sign-investment-facilitation-agreement-1762974.html.
17. "Military Spending: Thailand to Buy Chinese Tanks to Replace Ageing US Model", *South China Morning Post*, April 4, 2017, available at: http://www.scmp.com/news/asia/southeast-asia/article/2084725/military-spending-thailand-buy-chinese-tanks-replace-ageing.
18. "Malaysia to Buy Navy Vessels from China in Blow to US", *South China Morning Post*, October 28, 2016, available at:

http://www.scmp.com/news/china/diplomacy-defence/article/2041049/malaysia-buy-navy-vessels-china-blow.

19. "China Battles Fierce Competition and Quality Issues in Fight for Weapons Sales", *South China Morning Post*, October 31, 2016, available at: http://www.scmp.com/news/china/diplomacy-defence/article/2039880/china-battles-fierce-competition-and-quality-issues.
20. "Eyeing Maritime Clout, China Pumps US$ 27b into Port Projects, July 17, 2017, available at: https://www.todayonline.com/world/asia/eyeing-maritime-clout-china-pumps-s27b-port-projects.
21. "India Plans Closer ASEAN Ties to Counter China", *Hindustan Times,* January 25, 2018, available at: https://www.hindustantimes.com/india-news/india-plans-closer-asean-ties-to-counter-china/story-Argwkl2JGhUD4ERVzbEmcJ.html.
22. "Intra ASEAN Trade Outlook: ASEAN Relations with India, China and US", available at: http://www.exportgenius.in/blog/intra-asean-trade-outlook-asean-relations-with-india-china-us-183.php.
23. "China-ASEAN Trade to Hit US$ 1t by 2020", *China Daily.com*, May 16, 2017, available at: http://www.chinadaily.com.cn/business/2017-05/16/content_29364521.htm.
24. Lee Hsien Loong, "Revive a Millennial Partnership", *The Times of India*, January 25, 2018.
25. "PM Lee Hsien Loong's Opening Remarks for the ASEAN-India Commemorative Summit Plenary in New Delhi, India, on January 25, 2018", available at: https://www.mfa.gov.sg/content/mfa/media_centre/press_room/pr/2018/January/press_201801252.html.
26. "India, ASEAN Target Swift Deal on RCEP", *The Hindu*, January 27, 2018.
27. "ASEAN Rising", *The Hindu*, editorial, January 27, 2018.
28. Remarks by the Prime Minister at the 11th East Asia Summit held on September 8, 2016 in Vientiane, Laos.

3

India-ASEAN Civilizational and Cultural Links

Asma Masood

In the 27th year of relations between India and the Association of Southeast Asian Nations (ASEAN), it is well established that both parties enjoy ancient cultural relations. Several manifestations of people-to-people ties existed in the erstwhile eras. These began on the basis of trade and imbibed themselves into ASEAN's religious, social, cultural and even royal fabrics. Today, these aspects form the basis for modern era linkages that are seen in tourism, spiritual tourism, education and Diaspora. Nevertheless, there seems to remain a missing ingredient. One wonders for how long the present day gaps will remain: distances created during the Cold War and the subsequent rise of internal political distractions, coupled with pressing concerns due to American and Chinese interests in the Southeast Asian region.

It will be studied in this paper whether the 21st century requires a twist to forwarding cultural relations between India and ASEAN. Perhaps, the two sides must use reverse psychology, by basing culture on the ongoing burgeoning trade and investment channels. It is clear that the obstacles to spontaneous cultural collaborations as listed above are not deterring the increase in trade and investments.

Debate may arise on whether culture and trade must be intertwined. The goal is not on these lines. Rather the modern channels which are created for the purpose of trade can be used for cultural communication. The growth of cosmopolitan mindsets must be capitalized on as well.

During these deliberations, the larger perspective of India's big power strategies in ASEAN region cannot be ignored. It is essential to examine how India can leverage its advantages of historical, civilizational and cultural ties with Southeast Asia. This will be seen in the context of balancing Chinese influence in the region. China has an upper hand when it comes to financial resources for soft power. Nevertheless, India's goodwill and potential offer themselves as promising phenomena for cementing the country's cultural bonds with ASEAN.

In light of these analyses, it will be inferred how to combine both civilizational and contemporary cultural factors to reap maximum mutual benefit for India and ASEAN in the coming decades.

Introduction

India's 'Act East Policy' witnessed a significant milestone in 2018–the invitation extended to ten leaders of ASEAN (Association of Southeast Asian Nations) to be 'Guests of Honour' at the Republic Day parade at New Delhi. The ASEAN leaders attended the India ASEAN Commemorative Summit a day earlier on January 25, 2018. Three Cs-'commerce, connectivity and culture' were top on the agenda of the leaders' meeting with Indian policy makers.

These three dimensions are not new to the India-Southeast Asia relationship. While the 2018 summit was held after one year of India and ASEAN celebrating 25 years of diplomatic relations, the ties between India and Southeast Asia date back some 2000 years. [1] One recalls the statement in a 2012 media report:

"New Delhi is looking to announce a strategic partnership at the ASEAN-India Commemorative Summit in the capital but Indian travellers have been building bridges for years".

-Ashlin Mathew, *The Daily Mail* [2]

Interestingly, the 'Three Cs' were seamlessly interlinked in the erstwhile eras. It was via the channel of maritime and land *connectivity*, that *commerce* between the two parties existed, which simultaneously allowed *cultural* gateways to open. This is a notable phenomenon that existed, despite the lack of technical advances of the modern era. Nevertheless, although ancient India-Southeast Asia trade was not a flourishing phenomenon, it enabled the transport of not only Indian settlers in the region, but also the conveyance of ideas, commodities and technical know-how. [3]

However, the number of migrants from India to Southeast Asia until before the colonial period was insignificant. [4] Despite this drawback, relations at the governmental levels flourished. According to Mishra, Brahmans (priests) were travel companions of Indian traders and took up the post of court counsellors while enabling political leverage of the monarchs in Southeast Asia. [5] In fact, Indian forms of political leadership, such as Hindu-Buddhist concepts of royalty imbibed themselves in the region by the seventh century C.E. [6] Apart from affecting the ruling class, the Indian cultural influence spread across all sections of the society. The Brahmans would interact with the locals as well; contributing to the latter's knowledge systems, namely literature, scripture and rituals. [7]

Thus, a cultural and civilizational semi-clone of India exists in what is today known as ASEAN. Just as flora and fauna species spread across regions retain their similar characteristics, we see similarities in Indian and Southeast Asian culture, where the latter has adapted Indian civilizational threads to its own tapestry.

Meanwhile, it is interesting to observe that in the ancient times, there was an ease with which Indian influences shaped the corridors of power in Southeast Asia. This was not sustained during subsequent time periods. Although a large stream of skilled Indian labour was pushed into the region during the British colonial period, it was met resistance and disgruntlement from the locals. The following Cold War era witnessed ASEAN taken aback at India's stance towards unfolding of regional dynamics. Nevertheless, both these periods–Colonial and Cold War–were a blessing in disguise for enhancing people to people contact. While the colonizers were responsible for bringing Indian migrant workers to the region and thereby creating a foundation for the modern Indian Diaspora, the late Cold War era was when new age communication technology began taking roots. This to an extent enabled the foundation for India's 'Look East Policy' in the 1990s.

A major pillar for LEP was China's increasing economic sway in ASEAN. Thus, the early 'Look East Policy' while acknowledging the ancient cultural linkages, did not stress on civilizational relations as a big power strategy. The new millennium however has new demands. India realizes that ASEAN is crucial for achieving rich trade, strategic and cultural dividends, hence the policy has been renamed 'Act East'. A big power strategy is also called for when implementing the policy. Crucially, an overwhelming approach will be avoided. Or else there is risk of causing a fear of being overshadowed amongst the region's actors.

Amidst these deliberations, it cannot be ignored that this is the age of cosmopolitan societies. The future rests on the youth or 'millennials' as the term goes. They are determined, focussed and feel responsible not only for themselves but for uplifting the society. They are achievers from a young age and are capitalising on the opportunities of the digital era. They are seen among both urban and rural masses. For example, the demand among Indian urban classes for authentic cultural products and organic consumer goods is spurring a revolution among the country's grassroots. Indian NGOs are also thriving on the e-opportunities. Ironically, the demand in India for cultural goods is yet to see optimum inputs from Southeast Asia. Interestingly, this is a not a vast difference from ancient times. The only probable sharing of arts is negligible, such as Indonesia's batik prints which are now common in India. Apart from this, there was and is only a one-way traffic of cultural influence.

In other words, there has been an absence of a concept of 'Look West' among Southeast Asian countries while trading cultural goods. In the bygone eras, Southeast Asians did travel to India, but to imbibe academic or ideological benefits, not to spread their own philosophies. This was seen in movements seeking to capture India's religious inspiration (pilgrimage to Buddhist temples), its educational opportunities (such as Nalanda University) or imitation of Indian arts such as "ceramics and boat-building". [8] These dynamics are reflected in the current age as well. For instance, co-operation between India and ASEAN is being intensified, including in educational and academic fields, through the promotion of people-to-people contact, and initiatives such as Youth Exchange Programmes (2007), Special Training Courses for ASEAN Diplomats (1992) and Media Exchange Programmes. India has also established Centres for English Language Training (CELT) and Entrepreneurship Development Centres (EDCs) in Cambodia, Lao PDR, Myanmar and Vietnam (CLMV countries). [9]

An aspect that demands investigation is why there is no record of reciprocation of cultural export to India from Southeast Asia. While Indian rulers like Asoka directed the spread of enlightenment to Suvaranabhumi (Thailand), there is no significant documentation of a westward wind of influence. One reason may be that there is an absence of a homogenous culture across Southeast Asian countries. India too has ethnic fissures, but these lied within a single state ruled by one dominant empire at a time. In Southeast Asia, cultural divisions were high, both within and between the less porous borders of states. The Southeast Asian countries were also subjected to a streaming queue of foreign invasions, occupations and influence. Perhaps this caused them to draw a protective veil of identity around themselves, seeking cultural solace within their own region. The cautious stance may have eroded their desire for extending their socio-cultural heritage.

Hence, while the technological revolution may have brought about greater connectivity in terms of communication and trade, two-way cultural bonding is yet to be consolidated.

Besides, a paradox is observed: India and Southeast Asia apparently do not share optimum cultural bonding in the 21st century. The challenge lies in how to address this cultural gap while reaping rewards on the big power front. Hence, this paper will focus on delving on answers to the following questions:

1. How can the cultural gap between India and ASEAN be defined?
2. What are the opportunities to bridge the said gap?
3. Where do the solutions lie for resolving the above cultural quandary while simultaneously projecting India's big power strategy?

Putting a Name to the Problem

There are many avenues of cultural similarities in India and ASEAN today: religion, art, ancient architecture, and food. Despite this, there seems to be greater awareness in ASEAN about India than vice-versa. Only few countries of ASEAN such as Malaysia and Singapore are well known to the Indian common man and that is due to these nations' attractiveness as job markets. Even several urban Indians are not aware of the concept of ASEAN, despite the individual nations of the grouping being well-known. The familiarity comes from countries such as Singapore, Thailand and Malaysia being popular tourist destinations; or Vietnam and Thailand being the source of fine cuisines.

Primarily, there is a lack of awareness of the cultural connection between India and ASEAN. Herein lies the problem. The Indian mainstream media would rather focus on the developed West for international news. It is not surprising that the name 'Trump' is well known to every Indian. A key reason being: money talks. Southeast Asian brands are not yet household names in the country. This is in spite of India-ASEAN trade having increased to over US$ 70 billion.

Thus, India cannot claim to be a successful big power if only smaller countries are aware of its presence and influence. There needs to be reciprocity of importance given to the smaller nations. The motivation for this must not come solely from third parties, namely China. There is a trend among the Indian mainstream media that Beijing's clout is making India shape its ASEAN policy. It must be understood that India-ASEAN civilizational ties have stood the test of time. It is only that the spotlight of intellectual discussions among the media circles and their audiences is largely on countries that make economic headlines. Nevertheless, this paper does not seek to blame the media for being the root of the problem.

In other words, the scope for the governments and the private sectors to work together to realize the India-ASEAN dream is yet to be fully achieved. Besides, in this globalized era where markets rule, there is a lack of branding in cultural aspects. This may seem ironical to some observers, that the spontaneity of culture will be tainted by business approaches. The reality is that culture will remain to be an intrinsically natural phenomenon. It is the marketing and packaging of this culture that needs to be refurbished.

Hence there are four aspects involved in defining the India-ASEAN cultural paradox:

1. Lack of awareness.
2. Lack of reciprocity.
3. Government-private sector partnership lacuna.
4. Lack of branding.

Capitalising on Culture

Firstly, the awareness issue must be dealt with. It is of no consequence whether India and ASEAN achieve trade targets unless there is a wave of discourse about their cultural relations among citizens including laymen. For this, the media will be a reluctant partner until trade ties reach higher macro levels. To address the gap, the solution largely lies in social media.

One instance is the case of Nur Amira Maslan, a young Malaysian woman who has created ripples on Indian social media circles and even made headlines in Southeast Asia. She lip syncs and uses facial expressions along with hand gestures to popular Indian music on YouTube and Face book channels. Her performance has even been noted by a top-ranking Bollywood movie star, who expressed commendation on Twitter. [10] One notices the similarity to the popularity of South Korean television dramas and Face book videos. It is clear that private players in South Korea are doing their homework in market analysis. They are appealing to the youth worldwide, who constitute the larger part of the consumer market. India has no shortage of marketing talent and its players only need to be pointed to the right direction of internationalizing social media campaigns in order to capture greater attention than the prevailing scenario. In addition, traditional websites can be supplemented with rigorous social media campaigns. While a website for India-ASEAN tourism does exist, it is yet to be portrayed in an appealing format.

Traditional media can be roped in as well. For example, a documentary series titled 'Indian Diaspora in Asia' [11] on a Singapore based news channel has captured viewers' attention with its vivid descriptions of Indian Diaspora making a mark in Southeast Asian entrepreneurship industries, restaurant businesses and sustaining the legacy of their cultural roots. Indian origin women who are foraying into pioneering professions are also focussed upon.

There is hence a need to do a study of how social media and traditional media spaces can be utilized to maximise cultural awareness on either side. This will address the issue of lack of reciprocity. It is not that social media does not have common platforms across the two sides. There are certain smart phone apps which allow people from different countries to register and chat with each other based on common interests and topics of discussion. *Kik* is one such example. It is unfortunate that such windows of opportunity which do not need visas or tedious bureaucratic procedures are not well known in either India or Southeast Asia. India is well-known for its achievements in the IT sector. There is no stopping its tech-savvy citizens from reaching out to their Southeast Asian counterparts and collaborating in developing more such apps and other platforms for sustained interaction.

There is scope for two-way cultural exchanges in numerous other fields. Ironically, a lesson lies in a literary body of the South Asian Association for Regional Cooperation (SAARC). SAARC may not have any apparent achievements to boast of, yet there is one success story–the Foundation of SAARC Writers and Literature (FOSWAL). According to its official website, FOSWAL is the only SAARC Apex Body in the SAARC region, which is working under the SAARC banner, projecting and strengthening cultural connectivity through literary and cultural interactions among the SAARC countries, for peace and tranquillity in the region, through people-to-people contact and dialogue. FOSWAL has been building bridges of cultural connectivity with all the countries of the SAARC region since 1987. So far, FOSWAL has organised 31 major cultural events across the SAARC region, including various cultural and literary events, festivals, or conferences on Buddhism and Sufism.

Moreover, thanks to FOSWAL, Pakistani writers entered India for the first time after the partition in 1987, while writers from India entered Pakistan in 2001. [12] Truly, this is not an isolated phenomenon. The pen can be mightier than the sword of hard power in binding India and ASEAN nations together as well.

One questions why only Indian literature needs to be promulgated in Southeast Asian countries. There is in reality a rich array of literature since ancient times in ASEAN countries as well. Take the case of Laos. It may have seen evidence of written literature only since the 16th century–nevertheless this was preceded by a treasure of oral literary traditions, including poetry and folktales, which maintain their popularity even today. [13] Lao literary works in ancient times had significant attention devoted to Buddhist teachings as well. In the present day, there is an extent of control by the Laos government on its literature, given the concerns of the communist government. [14] However, there is a prevalence of literary works on varied themes which could be of interest to Indian readers.

Reciprocity can be enhanced in other fields as well. Tourism is currently balanced in ASEAN's favour. 2019 has been declared as the India-ASEAN Year of Tourism. This can achieve long-term benefits, if there is concretization of the current consideration on easing of Indian visa norms for ASEAN nations, in order to encourage Buddhist tourism. [15] The importance of tourism cannot be undermined. The large flow of tourists guarantees the continuation of favourable public opinion. While educational exchanges and research collaborations are restricted to a chosen few, travellers span a vast chunk of people-to-people contact.

One drawback lies in that the number of ASEAN tourists to India is very less compared to the increasing outbound Indian travellers to ASEAN, indicating a negative connection. India's rich history and culture has been adversely affected by the limitations in communications and the barriers to optimum number of facilities for tourism infrastructure. [16] Another possible reason for low outbound ASEAN tourists to India lies in a simple factor: There is already a rich proliferation of Indian architecture, temples, art and culture in Southeast Asia. Thus, India needs to re-invent its tourism branding. For instance, medical tourism holds vast prospects.

Implementation of ideas is the key, and can be made to bring tangible results if public-private-partnership is brought to the fore. Governments can enable a bridge between research organizations and private corporations. For instance, studies can be commissioned on how to tap ASEAN culture markets. One way is joint ventures between Indian and Southeast Asian media houses which will allow increasing of viewership and hence cultural impact. Spotlight can be put on not only cultural commonalities but concepts that are the need of the hour. These include environment for business, tourism destination surveys, Diaspora studies and entertainment industries.

Another area where research is required is how to not merely sell Indian products and services in ASEAN but to customize them according to local cultural tastes. In other words, branding of cultural ideas is indispensable. For instance, Malaysian and Thai packaged food and drink products are catering to the upper middle classes in Indian retail markets. With their attractive brands and high-price tags, they are prominently displayed and appeal to the fastidious Indian consumer.

One may ask what relevance culture has to such scenarios. The answer is that there is a new cultural group emerging in the 21st century–the 'Indo-Anglians'–they are elite, educated, follow soft religious practices and follow cosmopolitan lifestyles. [17] Undoubtedly, there are such crowds in ASEAN countries as well. These persons are said to be not politically influential, but consist of the top economic demographic bracket. [18] Research can be carried out on how this segment will influence modern cultural mindsets and trends in India and ASEAN, thereby driving culture conscious branding on either side of the Indian Ocean.

India from *Big Power* to *Smart Power*

While the above business strategies have cultural contours, India's role as a big power needs to be highlighted. The position of rising economic power cannot be consolidated without winning the hearts and minds of ASEAN people.

The other big power in the ASEAN region viz., China, is not only appealing to the Southeast Asian youth with its low cost manufactured goods, but also via its soap operas and music bands. Thus, a positive image is being pushed for by the Chinese. However, these are part of a larger Chinese governmental plan. It cannot be forgotten that in China, soft power is an official, well thought out and institutionalized strategy. Even music bands' business is affected by it. For instance, Hong Kong based Cantonese singing bands are facing losses as Mandarin singers are preferred on the Mainland. This is due to the prevailing political situation. [19]

Hence, spontaneity is being 'rigged' in Chinese cultural outputs, be it music, television, film or literature. Any difference that arises with Beijing's authority leads to an official condemnation (e.g. Nobel Peace Prize winner Liu Xiabo) and local clampdown of the artistic work. On the other hand, India's cultural projections are more spontaneous. This too indirectly offers an advantage to India's big power strategy in ASEAN.

In addition, Indian policy makers and civil societies can pay attention to the differences in the impact of Chinese and Indian soft power strategies. This is not unlike an assessment carried out by private firms of their performance, or a 'quality control' measure. A brief comparison of Indian and Chinese soft power has been carried out in the following analysis.

India's soft power is seen to have an impact in the following realms in ASEAN:

1. People-to-state soft power: Indians are helping the country's soft power goals in some domains. This includes the Indian Diaspora in the Southeast Asian region, who are not only holding onto their cultural practices but also influencing societal, political, and economic waves in the region. This is a clear case of a non-state actor proving its merit.
2. State-to-people soft power: India's Ministry of External Affairs is undertaking schemes to directly benefit citizens of countries in Southeast Asia. This includes skill development, education, inclusive aid, etc. Skill development should not be underestimated for its potential. As Thomas Sowell has stated, "racial, ethnic, and cultural differences among people play a major role in the events of our times because particular people usually have their own particular set of skills for dealing with the economic and social necessities of life". [20]

3. People-to-people soft power: Inter-societal interactions are not displaying continuity since ancient times as examined in earlier sections of this paper.
4. State-to-state soft power: India's soft power is moderately effective at the state to state level. This is evident from the goodwill generated by high level leaders' visits as well as India's support for the South China Sea dispute to be resolved through peaceful means and according to the United Nations Convention on Laws of the Sea (UNCLOS).

The overall impact of China's soft power is analyzed as follows:

1. People-to-state soft power: Chinese Diasporas in Southeast Asia are helping trade relations between China and the ASEAN states. However, Chinese citizens are generally not seen as making an impact on other countries' governments. There is one indirect impact though. By supporting their government's policies, the Chinese are validating their leaders' policies with ASEAN countries. For example, accepting educational and academic references to the South China Sea being Chinese maritime territory.
2. State-to-people soft power: China is not displaying significant signs of elevating the people of countries of ASEAN directly. It is often criticized for disseminating infrastructure aid which negatively affects the local population in the recipient country, such as by causing displacement, environmental damage or not providing equitable share of profits.
3. People-to-people soft power: Negligible impact. There is some influence however in the entertainment industry.
4. State-to-state soft power: Significant impact. Infrastructure aid is one significant area. It is noted that Chinese businessmen across Southeast Asia contribute to reporting back to their home country on the kind of infrastructure that is needed in the region, and Beijing makes aid decisions accordingly. Hence, there is a business minded

stratagem even in aid. The reason that aid is being examined in a paper concentrating on cultural and civilizational relations is that it offers an indirect yet crucial channel of soft diplomacy and hence stronger people-to-people relations.

China appears to be aware of the soft power areas it lags behind in. Perhaps, the country has realized that it needs to change the notion that its soft power schemes are a projection of its own interests. Primarily, these interests are in line with the rising country's core interests such as its territorial claims and economic endeavours. In this light, President Xi Jinping has sought to shift the narrative of how the world sees China. In his 'Asian Civilizations' speech in May 2019, [21] the reference to common Asian values and the scope for cultural co-operation were highlighted.

Interestingly, he emphasized upon both the historical linkages and the modern day tools for enhancing cultural connect. His talk touched upon the need to conserve Asian cultural heritage in order to "sustain Asian civilizations"; this was juxtaposed with highlighting the importance of media exchanges, think tank cooperation, film and TV exchanges. [22] What is of particular importance in this speech is that he proposes how China can reach out to other Asian actors for enhancing cultural cooperation, thus denoting that this endeavour would be China-led. It is also derived from this speech that Beijing seeks to shift the pivot of global cultural prominence to Asia, especially China. This vision need not be a catalyst for India to have a reactive strategy. Rather, India can recalibrate its existing strengths to achieve soft power in ASEAN and other regions.

However, the ongoing stress on yoga and Bollywood is far from a complete solution to India's soft power issues. India can make a unique brand of smart power strategy, one that involves the convergence of marketing strategy and cultural spontaneity that will benefit both India and ASEAN. Interestingly, this was already prevalent in ancient times.

Centuries of civilizational interactions enabled the foundation for cultural bonding. Permanent markers of Indian culture in ASEAN such as art, religion, architecture and Diaspora are well received in the region. When this is combined with new age techniques of cultural marketing, India will achieve another three Cs: 'comprehensive cultural camaraderie'.

For instance, Flipkart, an Indian online shopping platform can tie up with ASEAN markets. For this to be achieved, a makeover is needed in the governing approach. It is not enough to launch government sponsored cultural initiatives. As seen earlier, Southeast Asian literature offers tremendous scope. The focus can be expanded to include contemporary literary works from either side, in order to understand the pulse of both Indian and ASEAN nations' 21st century citizens.

Leeway and incentives can be given to private players to foray into the cultural domain which enables greater India-ASEAN partnership. Think tanks and research centres in universities from both sides need to look into the possible avenues of cooperation in culture and how marketing of culture can be capitalized on.

A big power strategy needs to imbibe the facets of a smart power, by adopting a reciprocal approach. Or else there is risk of causing fear of what this author terms 'cultural hegemony', as is the case of US. A smart power strategy will reap richer dividends. India is already taking a step in the right direction by calling for an Indo-Pacific concept that is all inclusive, unlike the US approach. This diplomatic move will help allay fears in ASEAN that the Indo-Pacific concept could cause a rift among their two big neighbours–China and India–which could destabilize the region. Strong diplomatic, political and strategic foundations are equal partners with soft power while implementing the smart power.

On the domestic front, a smart power strategy for India is to be inclusive throughout the country. The southern states share significant links with Southeast Asia in terms of human resources, tourism and entertainment. They too are cashing in on culture.

For instance a leading Tamil channel tied up with a major southern brand for organizing an entertainment event in Malaysia in January 2018. [23] The recent bonhomie encouraged by the Indian government to Assam for strengthening India's ties with ASEAN is another case in point. [24]

On a concluding note, the tale of India and ASEAN's cultural relationship is timeless. However, that is not a reason for letting the kinship to remain symbolic. It has been seen in this paper how culture and commerce can combine to make a winning formula. ASEAN should not be seen merely as an opportunity. ASEAN should be viewed as a natural cultural partner, which in turn fosters optimum conditions for trade and investment. India in the form of a smart power will not pursue a winner's game. Rather, it would enable an arena where all players, including ASEAN, stand equal on the podium.

Endnotes

1. Bhattacharya, Abanti, "India's Growing Soft Power in Southeast Asia: Will it Clash with China?" *Institute of Peace and Conflict Studies*, August 6, 2013, available at: http://www.ipcs.org/print_article-details.php?recNo=4104.
2. Mathew, Ashlin, "TRAVELLER: Indians flock to Singapore as Government Warms up to the ASEAN Nations", December 19, 2012, available at: http://www.dailymail.co.uk/indiahome/indianews/article-2250772/TRAVELLER-Indians-flock-Singapore-Government-warms-ASEAN-nations.html.
3. Kaur, Amarjit (2008), "The Movement of Indians in East Asia: Contemporary and Historical Encounters", in K. Kesavapany, A. Mani, and P. Ramasamy (eds.), 'Rising India and Indian Communities in East Asia' Institute of Southeast Asian Studies, 27-48.
4. "India-ASEAN Relations", Ministry of External Affairs, India, March 2012, available at: http://www.mea.gov.in/foriegn-relation.htm?ForeignRelation_212.
5. Mishra, Patit Paban (2001), "India-Southeast Asian Relations: An Overview", *Teaching South Asia*, Vol. 1, No. 1, March 14, available at:

http://www.sdstate.edu/projectsouthasia/Resources/upload/India-Southeast-Asian-Relations-Mishra.pdf.

6. Ibid note 3.
7. Ibid note 5.
8. Romain, Julie (2011), "Indian Architecture in the Sanskrit Cosmopolis: The Temples of Dieng Plateau", in Pierre-Yves Manguin, A. Mani and Geoff Wade (eds.), 'Early Interactions between South and Southeast Asia: Reflections on Cross Cultural Exchange', ISEAS Publishing, 299-316.
9. "EAM's Address at the Inaugural Session of 2nd ASEAN-India Network of Think Tanks (AINTT) Conference, Laos", Ministry of External Affairs, India, September 2013, available at: http://www.mea.gov.in/Speeches-Statements.htm?dtl/22180/EAMs+address+at+the+inaugural+session+of+2nd+ASEANIndia+Network+of+Think+Tanks+AINTT+Conference+in+Laos.
10. "Malaysian Lip-sync Queen Kak Girl Gets the SRK Seal of Approval", *The Malay Mail Online*, September 27, 2017, available at: http://www.themalaymailonline.com/showbiz/article/malaysian-lip-sync-queen-kak-girl-gets-the-srk-seal-of-approval-video#cbzk1im1swrXi8Ak.97.
11. "Indian Diaspora in Asia", *Channel News Asia*, available at: https://www.channelnewsasia.com/news/video-on-demand/indian-diaspora-in-asia.
12. "Foundation of SAARC Writers and Literature-Apex Body of SAARC: Historical Milestones of the Journey", FOSWAL, available at: http://www.foundationsaarcwriters.com/add_about.php?about_id=2.
13. Koret, Peter D. (2008), "Lao Literature", Encyclopaedia Britannica, available at: https://www.britannica.com/art/Lao-literature.
14. Ibid note 13.
15. "India Mulling Easing Visa for ASEAN to Boost Buddhist Tourism", *The Economic Times*, February 10, 2016, available at: https://economictimes.indiatimes.com/nri/visa-and-immigration/india-mulling-easing-visa-for-asean-to-boost-buddhist-tourism/articleshow/50849967.cms.

16. Chirathivat, Suthiphand (1996), "ASEAN-India Cooperation in Trade and Tourism", *Journal of Asian Economics*, Vol. 7, No. 4, 743.
17. Pai, Sajith, "Indo-Anglians: The Newest and Fastest-growing Caste in India", *Scroll.in*, February 2, 2018, available at: https://scroll.in/magazine/867130/indo-anglians-the-newest-and-fastest-growing-caste-in-india.
18. Ibid note 17.
19. Du, Wei, "Hong Kong's Cantopop Scene Withers as China's Music Scene Blooms", *Channel News Asia*, January 17, 2018, available at: https://www.channelnewsasia.com/news/videos/hong-kong-s-cantopop-scene-withers-as-china-s-music-scene-blooms-9867376.
20. Sowell, Thomas (1995), "Race and Culture: A World View", Basic Books, 1.
21. "Highlights of Xi's Remarks on the Opening Ceremony of CDAC", *People's Daily Online*, May 16, 2019, available at: http://en.people.cn/n3/2019/0516/c90000-9578617.html.
22. Ibid note 21.
23. Upadhyaya, Prakash, "Natchathira Vizha: Celebrities Galore at Nadigar Sangam's Event in Malaysia", *International Business Times*, January 6 2018, available at: http://www.ibtimes.co.in/natchathira-vizha-live-catch-updates-nadigar-sangams-event-malaysia-it-happens-photos-755813.
24. Choudhury, Ratnadip, "In 'Advantage Assam', Some See More Than Just Another Investor Summit", *NDTV*, February 5, 2018, available at: https://www.ndtv.com/india-news/in-advantage-assam-some-see-more-than-just-another-investor-summit-1808516.

4

Balancing China: India's Growing Presence in Southeast Asia

J. Susanna Lobo

The Modi government's proactive 'Act East' initiative—an extension of the 'Look East Policy—shows the Southeast Asian region's growing importance for India's foreign policy to achieve an influential status in the Asian region. The fast altering regional security equations, mainly due to China's exceptional rise, has drawn India into the Southeast Asian affairs to bring equilibrium in the changing power dynamics. In this context, of late, New Delhi has extended and expanded the range and scope of its priorities within the region—from the traditional economic ties to the security alignment—in sync with its larger strategic objective to ensure long-term stability as well as emerge as a 'security provider' for the Asian and the Indian Ocean region states.

By employing the 'balancing of power' theory, this paper makes an effort to analyse India's growing presence in the Southeast Asian region by keeping New Delhi's two objectives in sight: first, to counterbalance China's relative power in the Asian region; and second, to respond to Beijing's strategic encirclement of India in the South Asia region—mainly by strengthening its security and defence ties with Pakistan, Sri Lanka, Bangladesh, and Nepal—to cap its prospects to grow beyond the region. Since the beginning of 21st Century, India and the Southeast Asian states are concerned about China's power and its growing assertiveness in the maritime disputes. For this reason, their interests converge against the rising collective Chinese threat which, in turn, increases India's prospects to emerge as a long-term regional balancer.

Against this backdrop, along with its economic relations, India has enhanced its defence and strategic ties with the key Southeast Asian states such as Singapore, Vietnam, Myanmar, Indonesia, Malaysia, Thailand, and the Philippines. In short, this paper adopts a theoretical framework based on the 'regional balance of power' to analyse the scope and prospects of India's balancing strategy against China in the Southeast Asian region, wherein the regional states resort to balancing against the regional dominant power with the help of extra-regional challenger or an emerging great power, as well as to understand its larger implications on their bilateral relations in the foreseeable future.

Introduction

The rising power of China is a major development in the current international politics that has implications on the international power structure. Though China's power matters to the dominant power, the US, as it is not only challenging its global status but its growing power has security implications for the regional states, especially its neighbouring states that have territorial disputes. India and China are the two major powers in the Asian region that have major territorial disputes. Apart from the long-term rivalry, primarily due to their disputed territory and border(s), the two states rivalry has expanded beyond their bilateral issues (or disagreements) in the region at large. In recent years, the world's two largest states are competing and contesting for their influence in Asia. Both states have come a long way from their slow economic growth in their initial years after independence. In fact, their gradual economic reforms helped them to emerge as important economic players in the Asian region.

Since Beijing is involved in building a strategic arc of encirclement, India has also responded by venturing out of its sphere of influence to neutralise China in the Southeast and

East Asian regions. Now it is securing its interests by strengthening its security ties and defence partnerships with Chinese opponents in the Southeast Asian region. Given India's size and being a dominant South Asian power, its economic potential and overlapping political interests naturally make it a prospective challenger in the Asian region. To strike a balance in the region, the Southeast Asian states are also welcoming India's growing role to curtail China's influence.

China and India are behaving in realpolitik-way that might initially involve them into a game of balancing and counter-balancing and eventually shove them to a great-power rivalry in the region. While analysing these aspects, the paper mainly deals with Southeast Asian region where India is actively involved in balancing strategy to counter China. By employing the 'balancing of power' theory, this paper makes an effort to analyse India's growing presence in the Southeast Asian region by keeping New Delhi's two objectives in sight: first, to counterbalance China's relative power in the Asian region; and second, to respond to Beijing's strategic encirclement of India in the South Asia region—mainly by strengthening its security and defence ties with Pakistan, Sri Lanka, Bangladesh, and Nepal—to cap its prospects to grow beyond the region.

Regional Balancing: A Theoretical Framework

The common assumption of balance of power is that states tend to balance against the strongest power in the system (Waltz, 1979). While applying it to the regional context this could be applied to the strongest state in the region. Like the international power structure, regions too have their own power structures, the distribution of power matters among the states in the region. When a regional state becomes powerful and competing with the global power this alters the power dynamics in the region where other states would involve in countering its power in the region. The power of the dominant state in the region would matter to other states of the region. Apart from this, the growing power of the dominant state can have security implications for the regional states, especially for the ones that have territorial disputes and have rivalry. In the current international system, the regional states can be less concerned about the power at the global level and more about the power balance in the region. With the changing power dynamics, the regional states can involve in realigning their relations.

Apart from power, threat is also an important factor in balancing strategy, especially when there are territorial disputes and rivalry involved. The major development in the balance of power concept is the reformulation of the concept by Stephen Walt's (1987) balance of threat theory. The remarkable contention in this reformulated theory is that, states balance against threat rather than power which was a major theoretical advancement in the realist research program on balance of power concept. Apart from state balancing against the strongest power, Walt (1987) argues that states also respond to the threats from other states. Rather than allying in response to power alone, states indeed decide to ally with or against the most threatening power in order to balance or dissipate emerging threat(s). The regional states have threat concern apart from power that affects their security because of territorial and maritime disputes. When the regional dominant state increases its military power it is likely to undertake aggressive and predatory behaviour towards its neighbouring states. So, states are involved in countering their neighbour's power to have an edge over them on security issues.

States in the region can involve in balancing the dominant power by enhancing their power capabilities either through internal balancing or external balancing (Waltz, 1979). Externally, they can forge alliance or informal alliance to counter the dominant power. States do involve in balancing in the region when the dominant power strives to increase their power and influence in the region. The dominant regional power would like to maintain its position by counter-balancing its challenger in the region, constraining the emerging power by maximising the security cost and balancing through its rivals.

On the other hand, the balancing can occur against a dominant power when it threatens or is likely to threaten its neighbours with its aggressive behaviour or involve in expanding its influence in the region. To counter the dominant power, generally the regional states involve in balancing with the help of those states which are concerned about the dominant state's power and threat in the region. According to T.V. Paul (2004: 7), in order to counter the stronger states, states can form balances with or without the association of extra-regional great powers. Regional balancing can take place in two ways: (a) states in the region may use the global dominant power to balance a regional threat; or (b) states may align among the states within the region to counter a dominant threatening state.

India's Policy towards Southeast Asia

India has cultural, social and historical linkages with Southeast Asia with large presence of Indian Diaspora in the region. These linkages have played an important role in building relations with the region, but the economic and political differences kept them at arms distance during much of the Cold War period (Singh, 2011). Indian Prime Minister Nehru had a vision for Asian solidarity and freeing the region from the colonial rule and Western influence, these interests converged with the Southeast Asian states through the Bandung Conference. But once they gained independence, their national interest diverged from that of India, largely affected by the Cold War politics (Yong and Mun, 2009).

During the Cold War, India's association with the Soviet Union had made the non-communist Southeast Asian states suspicious of India's intensions. Thus, they, mainly Indonesia, Malaysia, Thailand, and the Philippines, distanced themselves from it. Another issue which also played its part was India's support to Vietnam's intervention in Cambodia. As it was against the great powers-led bloc politics, India did not see the formation of the Association of Southeast Asian Nations (ASEAN) favourably—it suspected the Western powers hand in its formation to achieve their Cold War objectives. The ASEAN was formed in a time when the Vietnam war spread within Cambodia and the non-communist Southeast Asian states saw its formation as a means to neutralise the increasing communist influence in the region (Yong and Mun 2009: 22). Differences in their strategic interests during the Cold War drew India and the ASEAN states apart (Yong and Mun 2009: 23). Vietnam's unconditional withdrawal from Cambodia in 1989, coupled with the end of the Cold War, created favourable conditions for India to re-establish its cordial relations with the Southeast Asian states (Batabyal, 2006).

In the early post-Cold War years, the economic dynamic of the Southeast Asian states was so impressive that India's new found economic structuring, that is, the liberalisation of its socialist economy, found merit in their transformation. Under Prime Minister P.V. Narasimha Rao's leadership, India launched the 'Look East Policy' in 1992 to engage the Southeast Asian states to give strength to its economic liberalisation program that direly required not only trade expansion to the region but also foreign investment to the strained Indian market. According to Tan Tai Yong and See Chak Mun, "it was the gradual convergence of interests, both in security and economic terms, in the post-Cold War period that motivated and underpinned India's 'Look East' approach" (2009: 25). India's 'Look East Policy' is the most influential approach that cuts into China's backyard in Southeast Asia.

After the end of the Cold War, India's engagement with the ASEAN has increased its presence and engagement in the region which started with its sectoral dialogue partner status in 1992 (Yong and Mun, 2009; Mohan, 2008: 45). With Singapore Prime Minister Goh Chok Tong's deft initiative, India was elevated to the status of a full dialogue partner in 1995, followed by India's entry in the ASEAN Regional Forum (ARF) in 1996. Singapore has played an instrumental role to expand India's role in Southeast Asia as it recognised India as a "natural security provider to the region" (Brewster, 2013: 152).

In 2002, India became a summit level partner with the ASEAN which accelerating its relations and presence in the region (Batabyal, 2006). India's encounter with the ASEAN has gone a long way from the sectoral dialogue partnership in the mid-1990s to the membership of East Asia Summit in 2005 where C. Raja Mohan argues, "India's Look East policy advanced steadily and became one of the most organised components of its external relations" (2008: 45, 2012: 93). India's entry into the East Asian Summit (EAS) helped it to develop ties with the key Southeast Asian states—such as Indonesia, Malaysia, Thailand, Singapore, and Myanmar—which are located close to its maritime border on the northeast of the Indian Ocean (Brewster, 2013).

In the late 1990s, India's growing economic and energy requirements led it to extend its neighbourhood conception beyond the South Asian region, stretching from East Africa and to East Asia to Australia, mostly dubbed as the Phase-II of 'Look East Policy' (Annual Report, Ministry of External Affairs, 2003-04: 38). The succeeding BJP and Congress governments knitted this concept to their foreign policy and expanded India's concerns and interactions beyond South Asia to the extended neighbourhood. With the extension of its neighbourhood, India has enhanced its 'Look East Policy' and entered into the second phase of the policy. The new phase of the 'Look East Policy', besides strengthening economic relations, gives stress to defence and security cooperation. During his speech on 'Resurgent India in Asia' at Harvard University, the then External Affairs Minister Yashwant Sinha opined:

"The new phase of Look East Policy is characterised by an expanded definition of 'East', extending from Australia to East Asia, with ASEAN at its core. The new phase also marks a shift from trade to wider economic and security issues, including joint efforts to protect the sea-lanes and coordinate counter-terrorism activities" (2003).

Likewise, Foreign Secretary Shiv Shankar Menon's (2007) address to the British audiences also emphasised the security dimension of the second phase of Look East Policy: "as we move beyond Southern Asia to India's extended neighbourhood…from the broader perspective, we regard our security as lying in a neighbourhood of widening concentric circles". In other words, as David Scott notes, "India's vision of extended neighbourhood involves power projection by India" (2009: 107).

During the 12th ASEAN-India Summit in 2014 held in Nay Pyi Taw in Myanmar the Modi government has transformed the 'Look East Policy' into 'Act East Policy', which prioritises India's defence and security relations with the ASEAN states. During the ASEAN-India Summit, Prime Minister Narendra Modi said, "A new era of economic development, industrialisation and trade has begun in India. Externally, India's 'Look East Policy' has become 'Act East Policy'.

Through this, New Delhi has stressed on more of action-oriented policy that would strengthen its ties with the Southeast Asia. This policy is of far greater geographical scope and its strategical depth while compared to 'Look East Policy' creating space for a strategic vision of Asia-Pacific (Palit, 2016: 82-83, Bajpayee, 2017: 360). India's 'Act East Policy' comes at a time when there are geopolitical changes in the Indo-Pacific region with the growing assertiveness of China in the region. In order to strengthen its 'Act East Policy', Prime Minister Modi visited the Southeast Asian states of Indonesia, Malaysia, and Singapore in 2018.

Convergence of India and Southeast Asian States' Interests vis-à-vis China

India and Southeast Asian states have long historical ties and cultural linkages but in the recent years the strategic ties are gaining prominence. India and many of the Southeast

Asian states interest converge in the region that has made them to collaborate in the strategic and security cooperation. Undoubtedly, China has played an important role in recent years for India to increase its security ties apart from the economic one. Scholars like Mohanmmed Ayoob (1990: 9) argued that the emergence of China as a major power in Asia has increased the strategic importance of Southeast Asia in India's foreign policy. Likewise David Brewster (2011: 226) argues that, "India's strategic approach to Southeast Asia currently involves a significant element of balancing against China's growing economic and political influence".

India has major border issues with China on the eastern sector in Arunachal Pradesh and on the western sector in Aksai Chin. In the last few years, there are growing number of incursions along with infrastructure and military build-up along the borders, both at Arunachal Pradesh and Aksai Chin area. With China's rise, its claim over the disputed border has been vigorous and assertive and has re-invoked the previous settled disputes or agreements. Apart from this, China is increasing its presence and influence in South Asia and Indian Ocean region. At present, China is not merely a rising Asian power, it also aspires to become a global power.

Against this backdrop, China is consistently expanding its power and influence in the region which is likely to clash or overlap with India and other Asian states interests. In the recent years, China has been involved in an aggressive encirclement of India—mainly by strengthening its security and defence ties with Pakistan, Sri Lanka, Bangladesh, and Nepal—to limit its growing influence and power in the Asian region. By engaging with India's neighbours, who are somehow concerned with its dominant position in the subcontinent, China is creating more issues and troubles for India in the region. In order to counter this, India is increasing its presence in China's backyard in Southeast Asia.

The Southeast Asian states are concerned about the growing power of China in the region and its security implications. There have been unresolved maritime disputes and contestation between China and the regional states on two major islands, the Paracel and Spratly islands in South China Sea. Beijing's growing interest in the South China Sea is facilitated by expanding its presence by involving itself in the construction of artificial islands. It has constructed seven artificial islands on top of submerged reef in the Spratly Islands expanding the existing Cuarteron, Fiery Cross, Gaven, Hughes, Johnson South, Mischief and Subi reefs into islands, while also enlarging Woody Island in the Paracels Islands (Military Balance, 2016: 211).

The artificial islands have facilities of military airstrips, radar equipments and paramilitary forces. China's assertiveness was witnessed when Beijing outright rejected the Permanent Court of Arbitration (PAC) ruling on South China Sea that was against China's claims. Beijing has continued with the activities in the disputed territories and has been conducting military exercises. This makes the states to support each other against the common challenger and threatening power in the region.

Economically, the Southeast Asian states' relations are stronger with China than India. China's trade with ASEAN is quite large compared to India. For the year 2016-17, India's trade with ASEAN was US$ 71 billion where as China's was US$ 470 billion. The states need China for their trade ties but there is convergence of security interests between India and Southeast Asian states. China though could have exerted its economic influence to get closer to the Southeast Asian states that would have made its peripheral area safer for it in its global ambition of becoming a dominant power but the security issues is pushing the Southeast Asian states away from China.

The major concern is the maritime dispute in the South China Sea. The South China Sea is also important for India's trade with the East Asian and the Asia-Pacific states for transit through the Strait of Malacca choke point. China's increasing military presence and assertiveness in the region is likely to affect India's trade flow and energy resources as well as its regional oil drilling initiatives. In recent years, India has supported the Southeast Asian states on their maritime dispute when India is facing increasing incursions at the border. India's navy has been deployed in the South China Sea waters and during the ASEAN summits it has supported the states against China's assertive behaviour and claims. In 2004, India deployed a six-ship flotilla and again in 2013 and 2014 India deployed its naval ships into South China Sea waters (Blank et al., 2015: 64).

India has been supporting the peaceful resolution of the South China Sea dispute as per the international law and under the United Nations Convention on the Law of the Sea (UNCLOS) which is in line with the Vietnam and Philippines stand to resolve the dispute on a multilateral basis than on a bilateral one by China. Vietnam supports India's presence in the South China Sea. When China is being assertive over the disputed maritime territory with Vietnam, the latter has being involving India in the oil exploration. China has issues on oil exploration also where many blocks put to sale are being considered as part of Chinese territory.

In order to counter China, India's ONGC entered into a deal with the Vietnamese state-owned oil company in 2011. India's oil exploration is also seen to gain diplomatic support for Vietnam's South China Sea territorial claims (Blank et al., 2015: 92). This is countering China's activities in Pak-occupied Kashmir where India is claiming Chinese violation of its sovereignty. Beijing is against India's collaboration with Vietnam in the oil and gas exploration that it considers as illegal.

India-Southeast Asia Defence and Strategic Ties

Over the last decade, India has enhanced its security and defence with the Southeast and East Asian states of Singapore, Vietnam, Indonesia, Malaysia, Thailand, Myanmar, the Philippines, and Japan. India's naval modernisation, which began in the late 1980s, has helped India to expand its naval deployment and maritime diplomacy with the Southeast Asian states, particularly those that border the Bay of Bengal and the Andaman Sea, through its regular port visits and assisting them in the Indian Ocean region (Scott, 2009).

Since the beginning of the 21st century, India and the Southeast Asian states are concerned about China's power and its growing assertiveness in the maritime disputes. For this reason, their interests converge against the rising collective Chinese threat which, in turn, increases India's prospects to emerge as a long-term regional balancer. Against this backdrop, along with its economic relations, India has enhanced its defence and strategic ties with the key Southeast Asian states such as Singapore, Vietnam, Myanmar, Indonesia, Malaysia, Thailand, and the Philippines. With its 'Act East Policy', India is further strengthening its defence ties with states like Singapore, Vietnam, Myanmar, Malaysia, and Indonesia. Rahul Mishra (2013: 104) is of the opinion that "apprehensions are that China brought India closer to Indonesia, Japan, Singapore and Vietnam, and subsequently, India signed strategic partnership and military cooperation agreements with all of them". According to David Brewster, India's defence strategy towards Southeast Asia can be understood in terms of two broad set of strategic objectives.

First, to be the predominant power in the northeast Indian Ocean and a broader objective to assume a greater strategic role in Southeast Asia and the Pacific. India's second set of strategic objectives in Southeast Asia stems from its desire to expand its strategic role in Southeast Asia and further into the Pacific. India is driven by an imperative to balance China's growing influence in Southeast Asia as well as its aspirations to expand its own strategic space (2013: 151).

Vietnam is the only Southeast Asian state with whom India had maintained cordial relations during the Cold War because of their close ties with the Soviet Union and this continued in the post-Cold War era as well. India sees Vietnam as a barrier to the expansion of China's influence in the region (Blank et al., 2015: 95). In New Delhi's counter-balancing strategy, Vietnam is an important state in the region as it shares both land and sea border with China and, like India, has undergone a watershed experience of war with China in 1979 and thus it wants India to act as a political and economic balancer to China (Brewster, 2013: 160). Moreover, their strategic interests converge as they are concerned about the growing power of China where Vietnam is witnessing the assertiveness in the South China Sea dispute, especially near the waters where Vietnam is exploring gas and oil.

India has been involved in oil exploration after signing an agreement with Vietnam in 2011 in South China Sea which had been strongly protested by China as it challenges Beijing's sovereignty in the disputed waters. India's ties with Vietnam are often seen as similar to Beijing's alliance with Islamabad to counter India in South Asia. According to Bharat Karnad, a noted Indian nuclear strategist, "by cultivating a resolute Vietnam as a close regional ally and security partner in the manner China has done to Pakistan, India can pay Beijing back in the same coin" (cited in Brewster, 2013: 159-160). With this objective in mind, India and Vietnam formalised their defence cooperation after signing a formal Defence Protocol in 2000.

Since the signing of the Joint Declaration on Strategic Partnership in November 2007, India-Vietnam security cooperation has enhanced. Vietnam is looking at India to strengthen its military might against China in the region. It is procuring weapons while its navy is getting training from India. In 2011, India agreed to train Vietnamese personnel who are operating Kilo class submarines and in turn India is being provided with berthing facilities for its naval ships at its port in Nha Trang which is situated near the strategically located Cam Ranh Bay in South China Sea. In 2013, India offered Vietnam a US$ 100 million credit line to purchase military equipments that included the purchase of four offshore patrol vessels that are built in Indian yards. With China becoming more assertive over the disputes and the frequent clashes between the Chinese naval vessels and Vietnamese fishing boats on the high seas, Hanoi is compelled to strengthen its position by involving in partnership with other states.

With this objective in mind, former Indian defence minister Manohar Parrikar and Vietnamese minister for national defence signed a five-year 'Joint Vision Statement on Defence Cooperation for 2015-2020' in May 2015 whereby both the states have committed to regular defence exchange and interaction, defence trade, training and cooperation in the development of new technologies. This comes at a time when China is investing US$ 46 billion in Pakistan to develop the China-Pakistan Economic Corridor (CPEC) to undermine India and Chinese airstrips and other military facilities in the artificial built islands in the disputed territory. India has also offered Vietnam its state-of-the-art Brahmos supersonic cruise missile to neutralise Chinese threats and in response Vietnam has offered India access to the Cam Ranh Bay to counter China's dominant position in the South China Sea.

India in September 2016, in order to enhance its relation with Vietnam, had upgraded its partnership from Strategic Partnership to Comprehensive Strategic Partnership in the light of the growing regional challenges from China. With this, India has extended a US$ 500 million line of credit for defence products to strengthen defence cooperation between the two states. This comes at the time when Vietnam is building up its military to secure its 200 nautical mile exclusive economic zone as China becomes assertive on its claims in South China Sea (Minh, 2016). Prime Minister Modi after extending US$ 500 million credit line said, "We have agreed to scale up and strengthen our bilateral engagement. As two important countries in this region, we also feel it necessary to further our ties on regional and international issues of common concerns". Without referring to any state he further stated that, "We also recognise the need to cooperate in responding to emerging regional challenges" (Indian Express, 2016). During the recent

ASEAN-India summit held in January 2018, India and Vietnam discussed on strengthening their defence ties and maritime cooperation.

India and Myanmar share border with China. India shares a 1,640 km. long border with Myanmar—with the North-Eastern states of Nagaland and Manipur. Myanmar is important for China as well as to India because of its geographical location. Myanmar is important as it is the only Southeast Asian state to share border with India and acts as a bridge to the region through road, rail and ports. For India, it is important for connecting with the North-Eastern states and for China it could provide as an alternate route to import its 80 percent of oil and gas supply for Middle East and Africa. It is important for the stability of North-East India in order to deal with the insurgency where the insurgents have their bases beyond the borders. In 2015, there was a joint operation targeting insurgents near the border.

India has focused its energies to strengthen its ties with Myanmar as China has developed strong ties with it over the years. For long time, India opposed Myanmar's military junta which ruled the country under 'State Law and Order Restoration Council' (SLORC), but Beijing's overwhelming influence over Yangon prompted New Delhi to alter its traditional position with regard to Myanmar's internal matters. India and China in fact were involved in competition for influence in Myanmar. China's increasing presence and influence over Myanmar was a major challenge for India in the region. Beijing is involved in development of Hainggyi port and setting reconnaissance facilities in Coco Island that affects India (Mishra, 2013: 104). In order to counter China's presence in the state, New Delhi has moved closer to Myanmar. Recently, India had joint warfare training exercise with Myanmar near Shillong in Meghalaya in November 2017. Prime Minister Modi in July 2017 described Myanmar as a "key pillar" of India's 'Act East Policy' and expressed its commitment to strengthen the bilateral relations (Indian Express, 2017).

Similarly, Singapore is an important Southeast Asian state for India, given its strategic location in the region, located near the Strait of Malacca, the maritime route linking South, Southeast and East Asia. Both the states interests collaborate to maintain security of the sea lines of communication for freedom of navigation in these waters. It is an important partner to facilitate India's presence in the region as it acts as an important gateway for India to project its military presence in the Southeast Asia (Singh, 2011: 45). Lee Kuan Yew, Singapore's founding Prime Minister played a major role in supporting India's involvement in the ASEAN and supported India's 'Look East Policy'. The two states' defence ties accelerated in 2003 when their defence ministers, George Fernandes and Teo Chee Hean, signed a 'Defence Cooperation Agreement' that provides for annual Defence Policy Dialogue to discuss security cooperation and strategic development of mutual concern (Blank et al., 2015: 86).

This agreement culminated in comprehensive tasks for facilitating annual defence policy dialogues, joint exercises involving the army, navy and air forces, intelligence sharing, and cooperation in the defence technology (Brewster, 2013: 159). India and Singapore are conducting annual naval exercises since 1994. Since then, the two sides annually conduct joint naval exercises, known as 'the Singapore-India Maritime Bilateral Exercise' (SIMBEX), that include the South China Sea as a zone of exercise. They are also involved in bilateral air exercise, codenamed SINDEX, "in which the Singapore Air Force brings its F16C/Ds to exercise with the IAF's MiG-27 multirole aircraft" (Blank et al., 2015: 86-87).

Moreover, Singapore's three armed forces personnel—the army, navy and air force—get training in India and all of its weapons are tested in the Indian firing range facility at Chandipur (Ladwig III, 2009: 96). Singapore entered into a agreement in 2007 to use the Kalaikunda Air Force Base for training purpose and in January 2017 was renewed for another five years for regular exercises. "In strategic terms", maintains Brewster, "access to Singapore's port and air facilities, in combination with India's bases in the Andaman Islands, reinforces India's position in the Malacca Strait and in the long-term, could even be used to project power into the South China Sea" (2013: 159). Singapore's prominent leader Lee Kuan Yew had stated that "India would be a useful balance to China's heft", for this reason, it openly supports India's role as a balancer in the region (Scott, 2013: 61-62).

Defence cooperation between the two states is strengthened in recent times with China's growing power. In November 2015, India and Singapore signed the Defence Cooperation Agreement (DCA) and in June 2016 they conveyed the first India-Singapore Defence Ministers' Dialogue (DMD). India and Singapore in November 2017 signed a naval pact led by Indian defence minister Nirmala Sitharaman and Singapore defence minister Dr. Ng Eng Hen. This has bolstered maritime security cooperation with access to each other's bases and mutual logistic support (Pandit, 2017). This will help India's naval operation east of the Malacca Strait that connects the Indian and Pacific Oceans and help in the operational reach. This way, India and Singapore can collaborate in Andaman Islands and Malacca Strait. Singapore Defence Minister Dr. Ng Eng Hen stated, "We want to see more participation, cooperation and activity in both the Strait of Malacca and the Andaman Sea" (cited in Pandit, 2017).

Indonesia is Southeast Asia's leading state with a unique geographical location which acts as a natural gatekeeper between the Indian and Pacific Oceans and therefore increases its prospects to emerge as India's indispensable regional partner (Brewster, 2013: 161). Since the two states entered into a 'Defence Cooperation Agreement' in 2001, on a regular basis, they are engaged in defence exchange and officers' training, ship visits, and joint coordinated patrols in the mouth of the Malacca Strait (Ghoshal, 2013: 70).

India also provides defence equipment to the Indonesian navy such as engines for its Parchim-class corvettes and repair facilities for Type-209 submarines (Singh, 2011: 23). In order to secure the Malacca Strait from external threats, India and Indonesia have coordinated naval patrols codenamed 'Ind-Indo-Corpat 33' for their shared maritime boundary (Ghoshal, 2013: 70). The two states have enhanced their relations in 2005 by singing a strategic partnership which provides them a common platform to discuss the issues concerning maritime and energy security, and counter terrorism initiatives (Chachavalpongpun, 2011).

Malaysia is important as it is also located near the Straits of Malacca. Indian PM Modi has shown interests in strengthening defence ties with Malaysia. In 2010, during PM Manmohan Singh's visit to Southeast Asian nations India had elevated its relations with Malaysia to strategic partnership. Though our defence ties are not that strong with Malaysia, recent years have shown keen interest by both the states to enhance their defence ties. All three units of Indian defence forces are engaged with Malaysian armed forces, with Indian Air Force team having trained Malaysian pilots on the SU-30SKM aircraft from 2008 to 2010 and Indian naval ships making regular ports calls in Malaysia (Roche, 2015).

Apart from strengthening its bilateral ties with the Southeast Asian states, India is also involved in multilateral initiative in the region. For instance, it is a part of the ASEAN states multilateral naval exercise, the MILAN—that also includes Australia and New Zealand—since 1995 which has strengthened India's maritime ties with the regional states as China is not a part of the exercise. India has also initiated the Mekong-Ganga Cooperation (MGC) in 2000 to forge stronger ties with Thailand, Myanmar, Vietnam, Laos and Cambodia. India is involved in Bay of Bengal Initiative for Multi-Sectoral, Technical and Economic Cooperation (BIMSTEC) in order to play an active role in the region which gives opportunity to look beyond SAARC which is often caught up with Pakistan intransigence. China has been a member of the ASEAN Defence Ministers Meeting (ADMM+).

Apart from India having defence and security cooperation with the crucial Southeast Asian states, India's Andaman and Nicobar Command (ANC) which is located in Port Blair is playing a crucial role in India's naval engagement with the Southeast Asian states as it is situated near to the region. India's military presence in the Andaman and Nicobar Islands is helping India to have military presence in Southeast Asia as these facilities/bases are closer to the regional states of Myanmar, Thailand, Malaysia, Singapore and Indonesia (Blank et al., 2015: 17). It is the only tri-service command with rotating three-star commanders-in-chief from Army, Navy and Air Force. New Delhi in recent years have enhanced or developed these crucial bases to expand its military presence in the region.

Conclusion

India's ties with Southeast Asia after the Cold War was strengthened because of the economic compulsions but gradually in the late 1990s, security aspect was accommodated in India's policy towards the region. In recent years, because of the increasing Chinese power and assertiveness, the Southeast Asian region has gained importance in India's foreign policy. India's 'Act East Policy' that replaces the 'Look East Policy' is a step towards this goal. Economically, China's ties are stronger with the regional states compared to that of India but security concerns are attracting the states towards India. China though could have exerted its economic influence to get closer to the Southeast Asian states that would have made its peripheral area safer for it in its global ambition of becoming a dominant power but the security issues is pushing the Southeast Asian states away from China.

There is growing convergence of interest between India and Southeast Asia because of Chinese assertiveness in South

China Sea. India's 'Act East Policy' comes at a time when there is growing Chinese assertiveness and activities in South China Sea. With the convergence of security interest, the regional states are encouraging India's role of an effective balancer in the region who also has security concerns with China in the region.

India through its presence in the Southeast Asia is countering China's growing presence and encirclement in South Asia. This is also strengthening its power and helping in its power project beyond South Asia. India does not have the ability or military capability to project its power far from home solely but by involving with these states, it can have its military presence in the region. Among the regional states, Vietnam and Singapore are playing a major role in facilitating India's role in the region. Though initially, Myanmar was closer to China but India's problem of insurgency in North-East and China's growing influence that could have implications on internal problems altered its policy towards it. India was compelled to maintain ties with the military junta. India's defence cooperation has strengthened with the regional states and in future would be influenced by China's activities in the disputed areas. The increasing Chinese assertiveness would compel the regional states to come together against the common challenger in the region.

References

"Annual Report 2003-04", Ministry of External Affairs, New Delhi: Government of India.

Ayoob, Mohammed (1990), "India and Southeast Asia: Indian Perceptions and Policies", London: Routledge.

Bajpaee, Chietigj (2017), "Dephasing India's Look East/Act East Policy", *Contemporary Southeast Asia*, 39(2), 348-372.

Batabyal, Anindya (2006), "Balancing China in Asia: A Realist Assessment of India's Look East Strategy", *China Report*, 42(2), 179-197.

Blank, Jonah, Jennifer Moroney, Angel Rabasa, and Bonny Lin (2015), "Look East, Cross Black Waters: India's Interest in Southeast Asia", Santa Monica: Rand Corporation.

Brewster, David (2011), "The Relationship between India and Indonesia: An Evolving Security Partnership?", *Asian Survey*, 51(2), 221-244.

Brewster, David (2013), "India's Defence Strategy and the India-ASEAN Relationship", *India Review*, 12(3), 151-164.

Chachavalpongpun, Pavin (2011), "Look East Meets Look West: Indian-Southeast Asian Relations in Flux", *The International Spectator*, 46(2), 91-108.

Ghoshal, Baladas (2013), "China's Perception of India's 'Look East Policy and Its Implications", IDSA Monograph Series No. 26, October, New Delhi: Institute of Defence Studies and Analyses.

Indian Express (2016), "India Extends $500 Million to Vietnam to Bolster Defence Ties", September 3, available at: http://indianexpress.com/article/india/india-news-india/india-extends-500- million-to-Vietnam-to-bolster-defence-ties.

Indian Express (2017), "Myanmar is Key Pillar in India's 'Act East' Policy, says PM Modi", July 14, available at: http://indianexpress.com/article/india/myanmar-is-key-pillar-in-indias-act-east-policy-says-pm-modi-4750520.

Ladwig III, Walter C. (2009), "Delhi's Pacific Ambition: Naval Power, "Look East," and India's Emerging Influence in the Asia-Pacific", *Asian Security*, 5(2), 87-113.

Menon, Shiv Shankar (2007), "India and International Security", Speech at the International Institute of Strategic Studies (IISS), May 3, available at: http://www.mea.gov.in/Speeches.

Minh, Ho Binh (2016), "India Offers $500 Million Defence Credit to Vietnam Seeks Arms Boost", *Reuters*, September 3, available at: https://www.reuters.com/article/us-vietnam-india-idUSKCN11905U.

Mishra, Rahul (2013), "China in India's Southeast Asia Strategy", in Ajaya Kumar Das (ed.), 'India-ASEAN Defence Relations', RSIS Monograph No. 28, Singapore: S. Rajaratnam School of International Studies, 97-124.

Mohan, Raja C. (2008), "India's Geopolitics and Southeast Asian Security", *Southeast Asian Affairs*, No. 20, 43-60.

——(2012), "Samudra Manthan: Sino-Indian Rivalry in the Indo-Pacific", Washington D.C.: Carnegie Endowment for International Peace.

Military Balance (2016), "Asia", *The Military Balance*, 116(1), 211-306.

Palit, Amitendu (2016), "India's Act East Policy and Implications for Southeast Asia", *Southeast Asian Affairs*, 81-92.

Pandit, Rajat (2017), "Eye on China: India and Singapore Ink Naval Pact", Times of India, November 30, available at: https://timesofindia.indiatimes.com/india/eye-on-china-india-and-singapore-ink-naval-pact/articleshow/61852056.cms.

Paul, T.V. (2004), "Introduction: The Enduring Axioms of Balance of Power Theory and Their Contemporary Relevance", in Paul T.V. et al. (eds.), 'Balance of Power: Theory and Practice in the 21st Century', California: Stanford University Press, 1-25.

Scott, David (2009), "India's 'Extended Neighbourhood' Concept: Power Projection for a Rising Power", *India Review*, 8(2), 107-143.

Singh, Bilveer (2011), "Southeast Asia: India Defence Relations in the Changing Regional Security Landscape", Institute for Defence Studies and Analyses (IDSA) Monograph Series, No. 4, May, New Delhi: IDSA.

Sinha, Yashwant (2003), "Resurgent India in Asia", Speech at Harvard University, September 29.

Yong, Tan Tai and See Chak Mun (2009), "The Evolution of India-ASEAN Relations", *India Review*, 8(1), 20-42.

Walt, Stephen M. (1987), "The Origin of Alliances", Ithaca: Cornell University Press.

Waltz, Kenneth N. (1979), "Theory of International Politics", Illinois: Waveland Press.

5

Deepening of Relationship between India and South Korea

Rose Veera D Souza

The much crucial strategic connect between India and South Korea commensurate with India's 'Act East Policy' (AEP) is forging new opportunities. Option to tap the technological prowess of South Korea and in turn the potential market advantage that South Korea is able to tap has secured phenomenal growth. The significant steps that both have taken to reinforce their bilateral relations in the recent years beyond economic sphere harbours new hopes especially as a balancing act against 'rising China'. The need for exploring new energy resources also gears up deeper engagement. The "unified strategic vision" that India needed to employ for a closer engagement with South Korea was tardy due to various factors, ideological itches and internal politics. Lack of convergence, procrastinations, identifying strategies and the vigour to execute the erstwhile policies on part of India have postponed deeper commitments. However, the AEP has demonstrated sufficient vigour and has also commended with its 'New Asia Initiative' from the counterpart.

Primarily, the paper focuses on the current relations between India and South Korea including economic relations, trade, strategic partnership, and the factors forging the deepening of the relationship. Secondly, it edges on the efforts that India has taken to establish bilateral relations and in promoting sustained policies to act in this direction. Third, it attempts to unravel the nuances of security equations vis-à-vis 'growing presence of China'. The attempt is to study the trajectory of deepening bilateral relations between the two and the forthcoming trends it displays in contextualising AEP. The reference to the centrality of India as the architecture in the Asia-Pacific vis-à-vis the factor of 'growing presence of China' is viewed.

Introduction

The AEP, popularised to engage India into its immediate neighbourhood, to the extended Pacific region, considers South Korea, a considerable partner. Prime Minister Modi's visit to Korea in May 2015 reiterated the goals of deepening partnership, by strengthening the erstwhile Comprehensive Economic Partnership Agreement (CEPA) entered in 2010. Both the leaders commend on the value of their relationship in bringing peace, stability and security in the Asia-Pacific region. While India appreciated the Korean Northeast Asia Peace and Cooperation Initiative (NAPCI) to enhance cooperation and security among countries in the Asia-Pacific region efforts to find complementarities between NAPCI and AEP to achieve the shared goals was enunciated.

Historical Antecedents of India's AEP and its Significance to South Korean Partnership

Though India's interest in Southeast Asia is traced back to antiquity, [1] its links to AEP are not very old. The vision of India to be a meaningful player in the Asia-Pacific region through a coherent policy towards 'immediate neighbourhood' comprising of South Asia and its 'extended' and 'enabling' neighbourhood in the Southeast and of Asia-Pacific region' could be traced back to Nehruvian era. To avail a better perspective on its trajectory, we have considered classifying them into four phases:

Phase of Vision: The erstwhile links of AEP could be traced back to the nationalist struggle of India and also to the common quest for decolonisation in the region. India's zeal to be a regional architecture dates back to the articulations of

Prime Minister Jawaharlal Nehru. He said, "The Pacific is likely to take the place of Atlantic in the future as the nerve centre of the world. Though not directly a Pacific state, India will inevitably exercise an important influence there. India will also develop as the centre of economic political activity in the Indian Ocean area, in Southeast Asia, right up to the Middle East" (Nehru, 1946: 536). Nehru's vision for Asian unity and regional spirit against great power intervention laid a considerable foundation and promoted the idea of Asia as 'one region'. As India was the second Asiatic country to secure freedom, it displayed the vigour to wield considerable influence on Southeast Asiatic countries in their struggle for freedom. In fact, the Non-Alignment Movement (NAM) also stemmed from the similar vision of unity and economic independence against the superimpositions of super powers of Cold War politics.

Phase of Inertness: The ingenuity of the first phase did not make strides in the next few decades, especially from 1960s to 1980s. [2] Much of it was also due to the ideological divide that guided the Cold War politics. In fact, India remained outside the Asia-Pacific regional organisations that emerged in this era, notably the Asia-Pacific Economic Co-operation (APEC, formed in 1989 and ASEAN Regional Forum formed in 1993). However, South Korea and India established formal diplomatic ties in 1973 and also concluded Agreement on Trade Promotion and Economic and Technological Co-operation at 1974; Agreement on Co-operation in Science and Technology in 1976; and Convention on Double Taxation Avoidance in 1985.

Phase of Renewed Vision: Initiative of 'Look East Policy' (LEP): In 1992, the then Prime Minister of India P.V. Narasimha Rao and his finance minister Dr. Manmohan Singh refurbished their outlook towards Asia and Southeast Asia also in order to assist the country fight its economic crisis. As a result, trade between India and South Korea increased exponentially. Besides, 1997 Asian financial crisis gave fillip to South Korea to increase access to the global markets, and to promote trade investments with India. India enhanced its participation by involving itself in Asian and Southeast Asian region and became a Sectoral Diologue partner with ASEAN in 1992, a full Dialogue Partner in 1995 and joined the ASEAN Regional Forum in 1996 edging on its 'Look East Policy' (LEP). Though, the initiative of 'South East Policy' under the banner of LEP made its debut in 1992, the term 'Look East Policy' was mentioned for the first time in the Annual Report of the Ministry of External Affairs in 1996. [3]

The first focus of LEP was the Association of Southeast Asian Nations (ASEAN) and its member countries, particularly Malaysia, Singapore, Thailand, Indonesia and Burma and later enhancing India's engagement with its eastern neighbours to include Vietnam, Cambodia, South Korea and Japan. The building up of relations were geared up through high level official and military interactions that comprised of summit level meetings with ASEAN heads of state along with official visits, political and ministerial heads, and military chiefs.

Phase of Deeper Engagement: In 1998, Prime Minister, Atal Bihari Vajpayee intending to gear up India's LEP further gave fillip to the concept of "extended neighbourhood". Hence, the policy acquired a strategic phase and got extended to the countries other than ASEAN members like Australia, Japan and South Korea. Yashwant Sinha heralded the second phase of the LEP in 2003. As the first phase of the LEP emphasised on political, diplomatic and people-to-people relationships, promoted connectivity and enhanced trade, the second phase popularised strengthening economic relations, defence and security cooperation and relationships in other related areas. During the second phase, though the dominant focus was the economic engagement, it also started taking strategic orientation.

The present government under Prime Minister Narendra Modi upgraded LEP and called it as 'Act East Policy' (AEP) during the India-ASEAN Summit in Myanmar in November 2014, [4] strengthening its focus and furthering 'Look East to Link West Policy', envisioning a broader Indo-Pacific conceptualisation of India's region. [5] Through AEP, India is streamlining its relations to strategic partnership with ASEAN, Southeast Asian countries like South Korea and all the countries of the Asia-Pacific region. Substantially promoting herself into ASEAN Asian Regional Forum (ARF) and East Asia Summit (EAS), India is also engaged in Bay of Bengal Initiative for Multi-Sectoral Technical and Economic Cooperation (BIMSTEC), Asia Cooperation Dialogue (ACD), Mekong-Ganga Cooperation (MGC) and Indian Ocean Rim Association (IORA). 'Act East Policy' emphasises on economic cooperation, cultural ties and develops strategic relationship with countries in the Asia-Pacific region through continuous engagement at different levels and by enhancing connectivity.

Redefining the Relations between India and Korea in the Asia-Pacific

India's strong desire to promote Korea's engagement in AEP and reciprocated by Korea's desire to explore the possibilities of engaging India in its Northeast Asia Peace and Cooperation Initiative (NAPCI) is gathering ground. A couple of key level visits by India to South Korea to secure support for its Make in India project and South Korea's endorsement to it are promoting this friendship. The Modi-Moon [6] leadership is gearing up the factors for deeper engagement.

The Government of India has underlined the importance of the Asia-Pacific for India's economic development and has accepted it as a springboard for India's leap into the global market place. The focus of AEP on the 'extended neighbourhood' in the Asia-Pacific region also includes gearing up strategic partnership with South Korea. Culture, commerce and connectivity are considered as the three pillars of regional integration for which India has shown leverage in terms of culture and commerce. Connectivity is promoted through transport, technology, and cultural ties[7]—physical digital and emotional.

In the Cold War rivalry, South Korea was in the American Bloc. The hegemonic rivalry between two superpowers compelled South Korea to rely on the US and Trilateral Policy co-ordination with US and Japan. Even now, Korean National Division and Inter Korean Military Confrontation is a prime factor in viewing South Korean foreign policy. The relation between India and South Korea did not move forward due to Korea's preoccupation with major powers such as Russia Japan, the US and China during the Cold War. Besides, the geographic distance kept India and South Korea aloof, though soon after India's initiative of LEP, the opportunities generated in India as a dynamic powerhouse, attracted the vibrant South Korea. The robust human resources, comparative advantage of information and technology, large domestic market and possibilities for huge inflow of foreign capital in Indian counterpart, made a huge difference to South Korea [8]

The growing presence of China also gave fillip to South Korea's initiatives for bilateral strategic alliance, based on common value, trust and global peacekeeping positing a new room for cooperation between India and South Korea. "South Korea favours a coalition among democracies in order to balance the rise of China" (Chung-in, 2012: 212).

India and South Korea: Forging Relations

One can trace the relations between India and South Korea to the international crisis of Korea in the 1950s. In a letter dated July 2, 1950, Nehru said, "...we have decided to accept the resolution of the UN Security Council calling upon its members to help South Korea, the resolution called for the withdrawal of North Korean forces to the 38th parallel and for member states to South Korea to fight back the attack" (Khosla, 2014: 279). The support of India to the UN was criticised as being siding with powerful US though India made it clear that India's support was to promote the establishment of a free and independent government in United Korea, elected by the people.

India's LEP launched in 1992, construed on economic rather than primarily geostrategic imperatives, [9] widened the opportunities for deepening relations. The economic growth of South Korea is often subscribed to American patronage, though factors are well identified beyond American paternalism (Varshney, 1993). India and South Korea had more or less the same GDP growth rate in 1962 (2.7 percent for India and 2.1 percent for South Korea) with predominant presence of agriculture in the late 1940s, with low levels of education, almost non-existent foreign trade, low per capita incomes and material impoverishment. However, in the late 1960s, South Korea's economy went through a metamorphosis when India's economy moved at a much slower pace (Reddi, 2003). If South Korean economy grew at a rate of 9.5 percent between 1965 and 1980 as against India's growth of 3.7 percent, in 1991, it recorded 9.6 percent and 5.4 percent respectively.

Though the growth of South Korea fell by 3.4 percent in the fourth quarter of 2008 fuelled by global crisis, the South Korean economy, through timely stimulus measures and strong component of promoting domestic consumption of products and compensating exports, made a strong economic rebound. The growth rate of 6.1 percent was achieved, returning its economy to the pre-crisis levels. The growth rate of South Korean economy is expected to grow from 3.9 percent to 4.2 percent annually between 2011 and 2030, comparable to the growth rates of developing countries such as Brazil or Russia. [10]

In the cultural sphere, "Buddhism entered South Korea from China, during the fourth century A.D. Korean Buddhists monks visiting India became the conduits for cultural currents and not only for Buddhists tenets (Malone, 2011). However, the deeper engagement began to be pronounced only when

LEP was launched in 1992. Through a series of visits to the ASEAN countries, Prime Minister Narasimha Rao established "instant personal chemistry" [11] and was able to enable India in the South Asiatic region. It is well established as to how Narasimha Rao with the help of his prudent Finance Minister Manmohan Singh brought in a huge transition in the hitherto neglected policy for Southeast region. The broad objectives of the LEP of institutionalising linkages with ASEAN, with its members states and to prevent Southeast Asia falling under the influence of any major power were well visualised.

In its second phase of widening the horizons of LEP, Yashwant Sinha, the Minister for External Affairs in his address to the Harvard University in 2003 began to expand the definition of East extending from Australia to China and East Asia with ASEAN as its core. [12]

Complementarity of Interests between India and South Korea

The perception of both India and South Korea on 'growing China' is complex and multifaceted. The divided two Koreas' standoff situation and also North Korea's nuclear and its missile advances have posed a disconcerting situation to Korea due its vulnerability in Sino-American rivalry. China's engagement to be a dominant sea power in the near future produces an equal threat for both India and South Korea. [13]

In fact, South Korea is better placed if China and India have normalcy of relations as having them against each other could divert its economic interests. Though the historical and ideological orientations kept them apart, the economic interdependence has brought Korea and China together. China pursues an equi-distant diplomacy with South Korea as it retains political ties with North Korea. In 2008, South Korea upgraded the relationship between China by regularising their meeting through APEC (Asia Pacific Economic Co-operation), the EAS (East Asia Summit) and China-Japan-South Korea tripartite summit. The bilateral trade between them has grown exponentially.

However, the recent standoff between South Korea and China over THHAD (Terminal High Altitude Area Defence) had brought unusual economic challenge to South Korea where China banned the Korean goods by employing its economic clout. According to the Hyundai Research Institute, this must have cost Seoul US$7.5 billion or about 0.5 percent of its GDP in a short span. Sales of Hyundai and Kia autos plummeted, Lotte was forced to sell off its stores in China, and far fewer Chinese tourists visited Seoul though South Korean exports to China rose compared to the earlier year. [14] Eventually, at the ASEAN Summit in Manila, South Korean President Moon and Chinese Premier Li Keqiang met and reiterated their intention to normalize relations.

Trump's visit to Seoul and the attempt of Seoul to normalise the relations with Beijing brings out Korea's ongoing 'tightrope balance' between its two most important bilateral relationships. On the one hand, Korea is bound to its long time ally U.S., on the other hand, China, with whom Korea shares direct geographic proximity and deep cultural and historical ties, is Korea's biggest trade partner and is part of any diplomatic solution to the North Korean nuclear crisis. "China's patience, confidence, and rising economic power translates into growing pool of "soft" power, giving China increasing influence in East Asia and the global economic system" (Garrison, 2005: 23).

One of the reasons for the popularisation of AEP and the growing complementarily of interests between India and South Korea as well as any other significant country of Southeast Asia in the 1990s was due to the common perception of China's domination in Asia. India also has to manage the challenge that any regional hegemon faces. "One of the most important challenges for Indian diplomacy in the subcontinent is to persuade its neighbours that India is an opportunity, not a threat" (Tharoor, 2012: 119).

The need for India to consider an effervescent policy at the neighbourhood is well-defined. C. Raja Mohan argues that without stable policy in its neighbourhood no nation can achieve its credibility at the global arena (Mohan, 2007). Also as former Prime Minister Atal Bihari Vajapayee continuing the concern for India in its neighbourhood stated, "Friends can change but not neighbours who have to live together" (Sinharaja, 2014). As Mohan Malik argues, China has played a dual game in South Asia and North East Asia, and has continued its policy of destabilising the region by transferring nuclear and missile technology to North Korea and Pakistan. China's centrality is perceived to be a threat to India, Japan and so also to South Korea (Malik, 2012).

The economic challenges of the time in fact pushed India to promote strategic connect between South Asia and North East Asia. Korea has recorded rapid development due to its export-led industrialisation. India's foreign policy, promotes improving relations with East Asian Lands beyond the Associations reach with Japan and South Korea, as they are major sources of foreign investment to accelerate India's economic development.

AEP has acquired significance in such areas as cooperation on counterterrorism and anti-piracy, maritime and energy security, keeping open the sea lanes of communication in the region's waters and joint humanitarian relief operations. "The rising profile of China and India and unpredictability of their bilateral relations as well as the trilateral ones with the US will have greatest impact on the region stretching between the eastern coast of Africa and the east Asian littoral" (Mohan, 2013: 5). As both China and India move beyond their conventional maritime spheres by reaching out to waters, the conflicting threads seem to be expanding.

As China has shown greater interest to concentrate on South China Sea, India has shown similar interest in the Indian Ocean. South Korea along with Japan and China is increasingly dependent on the energy and mineral resources of the Indian Ocean influencing the strategic thinking of East Asia. C. Raja Mohan cites that since the strategic community world-wide begins to focus on China and India-Chindia, [15] the term "Indo-Pacific" and the conception of single underlying geographical theatre are gaining ground. It is also well argued to be "confluence of the two seas" rather than separating them.

Historical records show the contacts between India and South Korea dating back to the first century. [16] The cultural connect is also established in terms of Buddhism and their colonial experiences. The poetic composition of Rabidranath Tagore and the institution of Tagore award by Samsung Electronics Company with the co-operation of Indian Embassy recently, refurbishes such a connect. South Korean Democratic Movement also seems to have had its influence from Mahatma Gandhi's non-violence movement. The cultural exchanges especially the Indian cultural fest in South Korea 'Sarang' and the South Korean cultural fest in India also are promoting cultural ties.

Deepening Relationship under LEP-Act East Policy

India's prudent phase of LEP facilitated enormous opportunities for India's deeper engagement with South Korea. India eventually began to articulate the need for going beyond the economic sphere in pursuing LEP, connoting deeper relationships. In fact, Prime Minister Manmohan Singh declared, "Look East Policy is much more than an external economic policy: It reflects a changed understanding of India's role in the world economy and signals a significant strategic shift in India's vision of international affairs" (Tharoor, 2012: 185). The LEP has been accepted since its inception by all the Indian governments despite distinct ideological stances.

South Korea displayed enormous zeal on discounting the opportunities presented by the globalisation process in India and India began to realise South Korea as a potential economic partner. "For 50 years, South Korea's economy has grown by an average of seven percent annually, contracting in only two of those years. In 1996, South Korea joined the Organization for Economic Cooperation and Development, the club of rich industrialized countries, and in 2010, it became the first Asian country and the first non-G-7 member to host a G-20 summit", recounts Marcus Noland (2014). In August 2000, South Korean Foreign Minister Lee Joung-bin stated, "India and South Korea are now fully conscious of the new security linkages between the subcontinent and the Korean peninsula". Lee further reiterated that India and South Korea are moving to strengthen co-operation "for mutual re-enforcement for peace and stability between our respective regions" (Mohan, 2000). Both the states acted as co-convenors of the "Community of Democracies" in the ministerial meetings held in Seoul in 2002.

Both of them have evolved economic, political and security relations and have declared themselves as strategic partners in January 2010. The Defence Ministers meet in May 2007 subsequently accepted the need for accelerating military ingenuity along with the development of the two side's economic co-operation (Limaye, 2008). Both of them share a history of national partition and confrontation with their discontented counterparts (Pakistan and North Korea, respectively) and also have to put up with rising power strategist neighbour, China.

The Declaration of a Strategic Partnership by South Korean President Lee and Prime Minister Singh in January 2010 focussed on political and security co-operation. Agreement for annual security dialogue between the two countries and co-operation in the joint development of defence technologies were the two topics which became significant points for potential and enhanced cooperation between the two, as India's role as provider of maritime security to South Korea in the Indian Ocean was highlighted.

Bilateral Trade: As KITA (Korea International Trade Association) observes, the bilateral trade between India South Korea is accelerating. India's share in Korea's global trade was 1.75 percent in 2016, India's contribution in Korea's global imports increased from 0.78 percent in 2001 to 1.03 percent in

2015. India was Korea's 14th biggest source for imports in 2016 and its 6th biggest export market. Korea's trade surplus increased from US$ 1.98 billion in 2007 to about US$ 7.4 billion in 2016. Korea's restrictive policy towards import of primary agricultural products such as fruits and vegetables has been already brought to the notice of Korea by India in the annual CEPA review meetings. The need for diversification of the export products is also required to be promoted (Table 5.1).

Table 5.1: Bilateral Trade between India and South Korea

(Million US$)

Year	Total trade	Growth (%)	Indian exports to South Korea	Growth (%)	South Korean exports to India	Growth (%)
2007	11,224	22.35	4,624	27.03	6,600	19.3
2008	15,558	39.00	6,581	42.32	8,977	36
2009	12,155	-21.88	4,142	-37.06	8,013	-10.7
2010	17,109	40.76	5,674	36.98	11,435	42.7
2011	20,548	20.10	7,894	39	12,654	10.7
2012	18,843	-8.30	6,921	-12.3	11,922	-5.8
2013	17,568	-0.07	6,183	-10.7	11,385	-4.5
2014	18,060	2.8	5,275	-14.6	12, 785	12.48
2015	16,271	-9.9	4,241	-19.6	12,030	-5.9
2016	15,785	-2.9	4,189	-1.2	11,596	-3.6
2017	18,438	28.7	5,526	18.7	13,912	32.3

Source: As per statistics published by Korea International Trade Association (KITA), 'The Bilateral Trade between Korea and India' (2018).

Hence, there has been a huge change the way South Korea and India are pursuing their bilateral trade. The economic and political relationship between the two is considerably enhanced after broad ranging Comprehensive Economic Partnership Agreement in 2010 which covers trade in goods and services as well as investments. As agreed during the Summit meeting in 2015, India and South Korea have started the process of review, with an aim to comprehensively upgrade the CEPA. The Ministerial Joint Committee led by the Trade Ministers of India and South Korea met in September

2017 has agreed to establish a Joint Future Strategy Group to identify areas of high-end technological cooperation, working towards cooperation in the fields of standardization and conformity assessment to develop mutual recognition agreements and pilot project to provide Indian IT services to Korean small and medium companies. Four rounds of CEPA up gradation at the DG-level have been held so far (latest round in December 2017).

Defence Cooperation: There has been remarkable defence industry co-operation between the two countries since 2005. Some observers have called India as the "legitimate dialogue partner in any future settlement with North Korea". [17] Prime Minister Narendra Modi paid a state Visit to South Korea at the invitation of H.E. Mme. Park Geun-hye, President of South Korea on May 18-19, 2015. During the visit, they held substantive discussions in areas of mutual interest and have endorsed the rapid expansion and diversification of bilateral ties. Park's State visit to India in January 2014 has provided for development of bilateral relations in a comprehensive manner due to which the two leaders have enabled to upgrade the relations for special strategic partnership. [18].

The Joint Commissions led by both the foreign ministers address to strengthen the partnerships between Indian and South Korean institutions of defence education, including the National Defence College of India and the National Defence University of Korea. It aimed at activating the dispatch of military officers for education, strengthening of regular consultations between the National Security Council structures of the two countries on security, defence and cyber related issues; encourage greater cooperation between their shipyards for defence needs, pursue further deepening of defence cooperation through commencement of staff level talks between the two navies and regular exchange of visits between the two armed forces; and also hold a track 1.5 dialogue annually between Institute of Foreign Affairs and National Security of South Korea (IFANS) and Indian Council of World

Affairs (ICWA). Cooperation for stable maritime transport, possible joint business projects in the area of shipping and logistics, and promotion of employment of both countries' seafarers is evinced.

Maritime: "As India has come toward South Korea with its AEP, and growing evocation of the Indo-Pacific as a strategic maritime continuum; South Korea has come toward India with its 'New Asia Initiative', part of a wider 'Global Korea' activism". [19]. Maritime security is evinced by the growing importance of the Indian Ocean to the long-term prosperity of East Asia" (Han, 2011: 8). The Indian Ocean is of course India's strategic backyard, but as part of this wider outreach, South Korea also operates in the Indian Ocean (Alexander, 2012).The North East of Indian Ocean is a strategic space and India's strategic presence in the area enables India to control the sea lines of communication that cross the Bay of Bengal and the Andaman Sea to and from the Malacca Strait. Malacca Strait is a vital sea lane for energy supplies for countries like China, South Korea and Japan.

Shared Culture: Both countries have shown shared commitment to democratic ethos, and liberal international economic order as a part of strengthening their strategic partnership. The possibilities through the Korean NAPCI and India's 'Act East Policy' are building up bilateral exchanges, so much so also in the shared ethos of democratic culture. For example, the exchange of India-Korea Parliamentary delegations, are significant in this regard. President Park lauded Prime Minister's *Swacch Bharat Abhiyan* as an effort to transform India. Recognizing that, Saemaul Undong (SMU), Korea's successful rural development initiative in the 1970s, can make a substantial contribution to accomplishing the vision of Swacch Bharat Abhiyan. The two leaders agreed that both sides would promote cooperation to create synergies by combining their development experiences.

The ongoing cooperation in science and technology and joint R&D projects are being implemented in focused areas of renewable energy, materials science, robotics and engineering sciences and health sciences. The cooperation in space sector has many possibilities. The agreement between Indian Space Research Organisation (ISRO) and the Korea Aerospace Research Institute (KARI) to pursue cooperation in the areas of lunar exploration, satellite navigation and space science and application is enumerated.

The two countries have underlined the paramount importance of peace and stability in the Korean peninsula. In this regard, they expressed concern over the development of DPRK's nuclear weapons and ballistic missile programs, which is in violation of its international obligations and commitments. They urged the DPRK to fully comply with all of its international obligations, including under the relevant UN Security Council resolutions, and to fulfil its commitments under the 2005 Joint Statement of the Six-Party Talks. Prime Minister Modi expressed support for President Park's efforts to build trust in the Korean peninsula and to lay the groundwork for peaceful reunification of the Korean peninsula.

India and South Korea underlined their shared interest in strengthening global non-proliferation objectives. South Korea expressed its support for India's early membership of the four multilateral export control regimes, namely, the Nuclear Suppliers Group, Missile Technology Control Regime, Australia Group and Wassenaar Arrangement, based upon consensus within each regime.

Conclusion

India certainly represents great economic opportunity for the South Korean business. Both the countries are very significant and are located at the two ends of Asia, South Korea in North East Asia and India in South Asia. India's reliance on South Korea in transcending AEP by strengthening India's East Asia outreach is paying off. Accepting 'special strategic partnership' with India and identifying India as an emerging power in Asia, South Korea presents lot of scope to enhance special strategic partnership. India's "Asia-Africa Development Corridor after the conclusion of China's "One Belt One Road" initiative", goes on to say the regional edge both China and India focus to pursue. South Korea's aim to find ways to factor India as a possible partner in its broad Eurasian as well North East Asia Peace and Cooperation seems to be picking up with Modi-Moon partnership.

There is also a greater possibility for a broader political relationship. In order to tap on this relationship, India needs to grow in political prudence and promote modes to guarantee swift concerns and work beyond rhetorics. The areas of education, people to people talk, educational exchanges, and cultural promotion needs to be strengthened. The AEP has profound possibilities for both India and South Korea to edge on their geopolitical options. Both South Korea and India need to comprehend the strategy of China as a soft power and the US's complex engagement with China as Jean A. Garrison states, "patient player ready to engage in both co-operative and competitive behaviour".

Endnotes

1. Early Indian texts call Southeast Asia as *Suvarnabhoomi* and India's early interactions with Southeast Asia is traced to trade, and transmission of Hindu and Buddhists religion. Amitav Acharya brings in the debate of antiquity and the modern origin of India in Southeast Asia (Acharya, 2017, pp. 31-50).
2. Factors like India's engagements in two wars with Pakistan and its pro-soviet stance was not taken by the East and South East Asiatic region. See, Acharya Amitav, *op. cit.*, 2017, p. xiv.
3. "Annual Report 1995-96", Ministry of External Affairs, New Delhi: Government of India, pp. 7, 118.
4. Narendra Modi, "Media Statements by Prime Minister of India and Prime Minister of Vietnam in New Delhi", October 28, 2014, available at:
http://www.mea.gov.in/incomingvisitdetail.

5. Indo-Asian News Service (IANS), "India Needs Policy to Look East, Link West: Narendra Modi", *Deccan Herald*, September 25, 2014, available at:
http://www.deccanherald.com/content/432698/india-needs-policy-lookeast.htm.
6. Moon-Jae-in, President of South Korea also accepted the need for special strategic partnership between the two.
7. See Bhattacharjee, Dhrubhajyoti, Research Fellow, Indian Council of Word Affairs, Event Paper, titled, "India's Act East Policy: Problems and Prospects in North East India", National Seminar, Imphal, Manipur, January 28- 29, 2016.
8. Moon, Chung-in, relates, the opinion of Goldman Sachs "India will emerge as the third largest economy in the world with GDP size of $27 trillion by 2050, only next to China (US$ 48.6 trillion) and the US$ 37 trillion. 2012, p. 202.
9. After few unstable coalition rules, a Congress led coalition under Prime Minister Narasimha Rao faced a serious financial crisis, as the gross fiscal deficit of the government increased from 9.0 percent of GDP in 1980-81 to 12.7 percent in 1990-91. The GDP growth rate declined from 6.9 percent in 1989 to 4.9 percent in 1990 to 1.1 percent in 1991 resulting in rapid accumulation of internal debt.
10. Report for Selected Countries and Subjects, available at:
http://www.imf.org/external/pubs/ft/weo/2010/02/weodata/weorept.aspx?sy=20.
11. Taken from Jayanth, V., "Narasimha Rao and the Look East Policy", *The Hindu*, December 23, 2004.
12. See, Mohan, Raja C., "Look East Policy: Phase Two", October 9, 2003, available at:
http:// www.thehindu.com.
13. See, Lee, Dong Ryul, "The Rise of China's Maritime Power and its Implications for South Korea", IPSA, AISP, 25th World Congress, Brisbane, Australia.
14. See,
https://thediplomat.com/2017/11/south-korea-and-china-make-amends-what-now.
15. Chindia is the popular term coined by Jairam Ramesh, the then minister in India's government, indicating closer integration of China and India.

16. The accounts state that an Indian princess from Ayodhya came to the Kaya kingdom which was located in today's South Gyungsang province and became Queen Hur Hwang-ok by marrying King Kim Suro in the year 48 AD. See Moon Chung-in, *op. cit.*, 2012, p. 208.
17. See, "India-Republic of Korea Joint Statement for Special Strategic Partnership", available at: https://indembassy.or.kr/press_detail?nid=377.
18. Ibid.
19. See Scott David, "India-South Korea Strategic Convergence and Security-Defence Cooperation: Relationship in the Indo-Pacific", in L. Singh (ed.), 'On South Korea-India Strategic Co-operation', Kyungnam University Press, October 2014, pp. 305-329.

References

Acharya, Amitav (2017), "East of India: Sino-Indian Encounters in Southeast Asia", New Delhi: Oxford University Press.

Devare, Sudhir T., Swaran Singh and Reena Marwah (2012), (eds.), "Emerging China: Prospects for Partnership in Asia", New York: Routledge.

Grare Frederic (2017), "India Turns East: International Engagement and US-China Rivalry", Gurgaon: Penguin Random House.

Garrison, Jean A. (2005), "China's Prudent Cultivation of "Soft" Power and Implications for US Policy in East Asia", *Asian Affairs,* Vol. 32, No. 1, Spring, available at: http://www,jstor.org/stable/30172626.

"India Must Look East", *Economic and Political Weekly*, Vol. 3, No. 8, February 24, 1968, pp. 356-357.

Haokip, Thongkholal (2015), "India's Look East Policy and the Northeast", New Delhi: Sage Publications.

Khosla, Madhav (ed.), (2014), "Letters for a Nation from Jawaharlal Nehru to his Chief Ministers: 1947-63", London: Penguin Books.

Kim, Kwan S. (1991), "The Korean Miracle (1962-1980) Revisited: Myths and Realities in Strategy and Development", Working Paper #166, November, The Helen Kellogg Institute for International Studies.

Malone, David M. (2011), "Does the Elephant Dance: Contemporary Indian Foreign Policy", New Delhi: Oxford University Press.

Mohan, Raja C., (2013), "Samudra Manthan: Sino-Indian Rivalry in the Indo-Pacific", New Delhi: Oxford University Press.

___ "India's Neighbourhood Policy: Four Dimensions", *Indian Foreign Affairs Journal*, 2/1(January/March 2007).

___ "Look East Policy: Phase Two", October 9, 2003, available at: http:// www.thehindu.com

Mukherejee, Rohan and Anthony Yazaki (eds.), (2016), "Poised For Partnership: Deepening India-Japan Relations in the Asian Century", New Delhi: Oxford University Press.

Nehru, Jawaharlal (1946), "Discovery of India", London: Penguin Publications.

Noland, Marcus (2014), "Six Markets to Watch: South Korea, The Backwater that Boomed", *Foreign Affairs,* January/February.

Ray, Jayantha Kumar (2011), "India's Foreign Relations: 1947-2007", New Delhi: Routledge.

Reddi, Vidyotham Veera (2003), "The Growth Experience of India and South Korea: An Empirical Study", ETD Collection for Fordham University.AI3083155, available at: https://fordham.bepress.com/dissertations/AAI3083155.

"Report for Selected Countries and Subjects", available at: http://www.imf.org/external/pubs/ft/weo/2010/02/weodata/weorept.aspx?sy=20.

Sinha, Atish and Madhup Mohta (2007), "Indian Foreign Policy: Challenges and Opportunities", New Delhi: Academic Foundation and Foreign Service Institute.

Tammita-Delgoda Sinharaja (2014), "A Key to the Future Commonality, Divergence and the Path to Convergence", in Bhatia Rajiv et al. (eds.), 'Transforming South Asia: Imperatives for Action', New Delhi: Knowledge Books.

Tharoor Shashi, (2012), "Pax Indica: India and the World of the 21st Century", London: Penguin Books.

Varsheney Ashutosh (1993), "India International Centre Quarterly", Vol. 20, No. 4, pp. 1-18, India International Centre, available at: http://www.jstor.org/stable/23003687.

6

Promoting Vietnam-India Comprehensive Strategic Partnership

Tran Ngoc Diem

In 2014, Prime Minister Narendra Modi launched a new concept of "Acting East" instead of "Looking East", moving from strategic orientation to real action with stronger determination. With the important strategic location, Vietnam has been becoming a pivotal country in India's 'Act East Policy'. The fact that India considered Vietnam a key player in its 'Act East Policy' has created a space to accelerate their bilateral political relations, bringing a significant breakthrough in the traditional relationship between Vietnam and India. Vietnam and India agreed to elevate their relationship to the comprehensive strategic partnership in 2016, providing a new direction, momentum and substance to the bilateral cooperation.

Moreover, the growing reach of China's economic and diplomatic footprint in the region has been identified as a factor stimulating Vietnam-India cooperation. Thus, how has the context of the 'Act East Policy' been speeding up the comprehensive strategic relationship between Vietnam and India? To answer the question, the paper seeks to analyze and evaluate the impact of the 'Act East Policy' on bilateral cooperation and explore prospective directions for Vietnam-India relationship in the future. Also by applying historical analysis and international relations theories, the paper based on the reality of bilateral relations, evaluates the achievements in Vietnam-India cooperation.

The paper affirms that Vietnam and India possess a number of historical, international and regional advantages which facilitate them to develop a comprehensive strategic relationship deeper and deeper. The cooperation in political security, trading and investment, energy, culture and connectivity will be key factors in orientating the relationship between Vietnam and India. In the coming years, both Vietnam and India will together strive to achieve important targets set aside by the two countries so that a comprehensive strategic relationship becomes practical and efficient. According to the foreign policy line of independence, self-reliance and multilateralization of international relations, Vietnam has enhanced its relationship with India covering a wide range of issues while maintaining a stable relationship with China. Amidst the rise of India, Vietnam continues to explore the opportunities for greater collaboration with India and welcome a greater role for *India* in the regional and international arena.

Vietnam-India Comprehensive Strategic Partnership: New Developments

Vietnam and India share a traditional and close political relationship evidenced by long-lasting friendship between the two nations. Traditional bilateral relations are heritage and potential to tie India to Vietnam, especially since India implemented 'Look East Policy' and 'Act East Policy' at present. On the occasion of visit of Prime Minister Narendra Modi to Vietnam in September 2016, the two countries decided to upgrade their Strategic Partnership to Comprehensive Strategic Partnership. Accordingly, relations between Vietnam and India will keep developing intensively based on the comprehensive strategic partnership. Promotion of Vietnam-India comprehensive strategic partnership not only brings wealth to people of the two countries but also practically serves strategic benefits of each party in making contributions to its role improvement and enhancement of regional cooperation and development opportunities.

During Prime Minister Modi's visit to Vietnam in 2016, altogether twelve agreements were signed between the two countries. Besides boosting trade, economic and investment ties, agreements related to establishment of software parks and joint agreements in the field of health, defence and space cooperation were entered upon. Inaugurations of Indian Cultural Centre at Hanoi and restoration work of the Cham monuments at My Son have been significant in deepening cultural and historical links between India and Vietnam. Prime Minister has also invited Vietnamese companies to take advantage of the various schemes and flagship programmes of the Indian Government such as Make in India and Digital India. India has pledged to be Vietnam's 'partner and a friend' in its "rapid development" and "strong economic growth".

Cooperation in Security and Defence

Relations between the two countries have gained encouraging achievements regarding defence cooperation, including visits of leaders, annual talks of leaders, cooperation on defence equipment purchase, services and regional cooperation such as ASEAN Defence Ministers' Meeting Plus (ADMM+). India-Vietnam Joint Statement on the occasion of visit of the President Truong Tan Sang to India in October 2011 declares, "The two parties stressed the importance of maintaining peace, stability and of ensuring the safety, security and freedom of navigation in the high seas. The two parties agreed that disputes in the East Sea need to be settled through peaceful negotiations, without resorting to the threat or use of force by the parties concerned, in accordance with universally recognized principles of international law, including the 1982 United Nations Convention on the Law of the Sea (UNCLOS) and the 2002 ASEAN-China Declaration on the Conduct of Parties in the East Sea (DOC)". [1] In the context of increasing influence of countries in the East Sea, India and Vietnam have been sharing cooperation opportunities at higher level regarding navy and marine connectivity.

Defence policy in 'Act East Policy' of India towards Vietnam plays a role of strengthening the Vietnamese military strength as a result. One more credit facility of US$ 500 million was granted to Vietnam in 2016 under the joint statement on framework of comprehensive strategic cooperation between Vietnam and India. Besides, regular naval exercises between Vietnamese navy and Indian navy and diplomatic visits of Indian naval ships to Vietnamese ports are also important. In September, 2017, in a friendship visit to Hai Phong City, INS Satpura stealth frigate manufactured by India arrived at Hai Phong port with 65 officers and 580 sailors. These two stealth frigates are manufactured with modern equipment and are a pride of Indian Navy. In the visit, captains of the two naval ships coordinated with Vietnamese Navy to organize joint manoeuvres on naval ship arrangement in sea and sport contests with soldiers of Vietnamese People's Navy.

During the official visit of Chief of the Naval Staff of the Indian Navy, Chairman of the Chiefs of Staff Committee to Vietnam in October 2017, Admiral Sunil Lanba talked with Vietnamese leaders and kept stating that defence cooperation is one of important pillars of Vietnam-India Comprehensive Strategic Partnership. In the near future, two parties aim to effectively cooperate in various fields under signed agreements including Joint Vision Statement on Vietnam-India Defence Relations for the period 2015-2020. Military of two parties need to maintain and strengthen exchange of delegations at all levels, and pay attention to exchange of young officers, especially in education and training.

For nuclear power, two countries also cooperate in use of nuclear technology for peaceful purposes and a Framework Agreement on this issue was signed in visit of Chairwoman of the National Assembly Nguyen Thi Kim Ngan to India in December, 2016. Two countries have been cooperating in Exploration of Outer Space (Exploration of Outer Space for Peaceful Purposes) and signed a Framework Agreement during the visit of Prime Minister Modi to Vietnam in 2016.

Cooperation in Economy, Trade and Investment

Leaders of the two countries have taken many practical measures including promotion of established mechanisms such as the Sub-Committee on Trade, strengthening of cooperation between Indian states and Vietnamese localities, strengthening of delegation exchange and cooperation among enterprises, periodic organization of trade fairs, forums, events such as Vietnam-India business forum, and India-CLMV business forum. According to statistics of the General Department of Vietnam Customs, in the first 11 months of 2017, total import and export turnover between Vietnam and India stood at US$ 6.86 billion, increasing by 41.45 percent in comparison with US$ 4.85 billion in the same period during the previous year. [2] However, in order to increase bilateral trade turnover to US$ 15 billion by 2020, the two countries must take advantage of new trade and business opportunities. Two parties have many potentials for development of trade relations because in comparison with Vietnamese economy scale (nominal GDP of US$ 200 billion in 2016, 90 million consumers) and Indian economy scale (nominal GDP of US$ 2,250 billion, more than 1.2 billion consumers), the trade turnover above is still limited.

Vietnam keeps attracting investment from Indian companies. During 2015-2016, foreign direct investment from India into Vietnam was only US$ 9.4 million and during 2016-2017, this rocketed to US$ 18.8 million. [3] By the end of November 2017, Indian companies registered 168 projects with total investment capital of US$ 756.29 million. [4] Indian companies have been particularly investing in energy, mineral exploration, agricultural product processing, sugar production, agricultural chemicals, and information technology in Vietnam.

Some large investors from India in mineral exploration include ONGC Videsh Ltd. (OVL), Essar Exploration and Production Ltd., Nagarjuna Ltd., Venkateswara Hatcheries, Philips Carbon and McLeod Russell. OVL signed the production sharing contract (PSC) for the 7,058 square km.

Block 128 in offshore PhuKhanh Basin, Vietnam on May 24, 2006. [5] In July 2017, Vietnam kept on extending oil drilling and exploration by India in another area in the East Sea for the fifth time for 2 more years.

Besides, Vietnamese enterprises will be more likely to search new business opportunities in India by taking advantage of programs including "Make in India" or "Digital India". Both the countries have been making every endeavour to facilitate expansion of cooperation and investment among the enterprises of the two by opening branches of banks overseas. This is manifest following the opening of representative offices of banks such as Bank of India and Indian Overseas Bank in Ho Chi Minh City. In July 2016, the State Bank of Vietnam (SBV) licensed Bank of India to establish branches in Vietnam. Branches also have functions of providing banking services such as receipt of deposit from customers, lending in Vietnamese currency and other foreign currencies in Vietnam. Branches will also meet demand of organizations, small and medium-sized enterprises for trade support, payment services, purchase and sale of foreign currencies.

Based on continuously strengthened defence-security relations, India and Vietnam will gradually cooperate in defence and navy to support military modernization of Vietnam. An investment field with high development potential preferred by Indian enterprises when making investment into Vietnam is the shipbuilding industry. In 2016, during the visit of Prime Minister Narendra Modi, the government of the two countries signed an agreement amounting to US$ 100 million to build 12 naval patrol ships for the Ministry of Defence of Vietnam and declared a credit facility amounting to US$ 500 million in defence field. Through bilateral meetings, representatives of many shipbuilding enterprises including Goa Shipyard, Bharat Electronics Limited, and Larsen & Toubro showed their strengths as the best Indian enterprises regarding naval patrol ship design and building, and ensured to serve demand of their partners and assist Vietnam Coast Guard in all patrol activities in sea.

Cooperation in Culture, Education, Training, Science, Technology and People-to-People Exchanges

Vietnam and India have coordinated and implemented many meaningful activities. Cultural events are mainly organized in combination with events regarding political and economic cooperation. Among events for celebration of 45 years of diplomatic relations and 10 years of strategic partnership, on April 20, 2017, Embassy of India opened an Indian Cultural Centre in Hanoi. The Centre will make contributions for promotion of India and its people to the Vietnamese people and promote cultural exchange and tourism. Via this Centre, Vietnamese people will have opportunities to learn art forms, ethnic music, dances, songs, yoga and other art forms of India. Besides, events of Indian Buddhist Festivals in Vietnam (from March 16th to March 19th, 2017) were organized by the Buddhist Sangha of Vietnam in association with Vietnam-India Friendship Association and the Embassy of India in Hanoi. These events show cultural and spiritual ties between Vietnam and India through Buddhism.

In order to promote cultural and educational cooperation, Indian authorities have been offering many scholarships to Vietnamese officers and students in the framework of General Scholarship Scheme (GSS), Mekong-Ganga Cooperation (MGC) and Education Exchange Programme (EEP) under the aegis of Indian Council for Cultural Relations (ICCR) schemes. Besides, scholarships under the Indian Technical and Economic Cooperation (ITEC) Scheme are also being offered and Vietnam will be one of countries receiving the highest number of ITEC scholarships and other scholarship from the Government of India. India will keep funding US$ 5 million for Vietnam to build a software park in Nha Trang Telecommunications University. [6]

India has recently played an active role in human resource development and training cooperation in defence with Vietnam. Vietnam also considers that officer training is one of measures to develop comprehensive cooperation relationship between Vietnam and India. In May 2017, a delegation of officers and students of Indian National Defence University had a study visit to Vietnam. The visit has enabled academies, schools and research agencies of the military of the two countries to strengthen cooperation and exchange of ideas, discussion of experience and improving of mutual understanding and trust between people and military of the two countries.

In official friendship visit of Senior Lieutenant General Luong Cuong, Chief of the General Department of Politics of Vietnam People's Army to the Republic of India in 2017, cooperation in defence training and soldier coaching was concretised for development of bilateral defence relations. India is willing to facilitate and assist Vietnam People's Army in some fields that India has experience in. Exchange of delegations at all levels, cooperation in soldier training, coaching, exchange among young officers, cooperation among military arms, branches in training and coaching, etc. need to be promoted.

Prospects of Relationship between Vietnam and India in the Near Future

Under the direction of Prime Minister Modi, 'Look East Policy' is called by a new impressive term–'Act East Policy'. This term was notably mentioned for the first time in the third Round table of ASEAN-India Network of Think-Tanks in August 2014 when the Minister of External Affairs for India said that India not only "looked East" but also "acted East". Inherited from the policy in the 1990s, at present, 'Look East Policy' has been transformed into a new age of expanding relations to the East based on policies in the past and internal strategies as well as emerging of regional ties with presence of

China. The Government of India shows its aim of playing a greater role in the region. [7] This shows a significant ambition of India to upgrade its relations with Eastern countries, including ASEAN and the Northeast Asia.

An important adjustment of 'Act East Policy' in comparison with 'Look East Policy' is more attention to the East Sea. Under directions of Prime Minister Modi, in order to strengthen relations with Vietnam in the framework of 'Act East Policy', India has described itself as a country playing a reliable security role in the region. When giving opinions on disputes in the East Sea, India has made progress when directly giving opinions on necessity for settlement of disputes in sea and emphasizing marine security, instead of witnessing this issue. With awareness of the fact that it is necessary to make practical actions instead of only looking East, India-ASEAN relations in general and India-Vietnam in particular will gain new heights. This results from the key role, Vietnam would play in the 'Act East Policy' determined by the Government of India. India has become more outspoken on maritime and territorial disputes in East Asia.

In joint statements with high-level officials from the Philippines and Vietnam, India has come out and explicitly called for the resolution of all disputes in a peaceful manner in accordance with the international law. The Indian Navy has also recently expanded its military-to-military contacts with various Southeast Asian states. Located in an important and strategic geographical position and having potential for improving influences in the Southeast Asia through economic development in recent years, Vietnam is able to play a key role in relations between India and ASEAN, assisting India in materializing targets of the 'Act East Policy'.

On the occasion of the visit of the Minister of Foreign Affairs Pham Binh Minh to India in July 2017, former Minister of External Affairs Sushma Swaraj re-declared commitment of India to implementing the 'Act East Policy' more effectively, in which, considering ASEAN in general and

Vietnam in particular as the centre points. [8] Strategic partnership based on five main pillars between the two countries will be further strengthened and developed to benefit the two countries, especially in security and defence cooperation. The completion of 25 years of India-ASEAN dialogue partnership, with a commemorative summit held on January 25, 2018, during which India showcased its 'Act East Policy', focused on fostering trade and other relationships with ASEAN countries, besides developing India's North-East, seen as a gateway to its engagement with the region. Vietnam is an integral member of ASEAN and a significant leg in augmenting India's 'Act East Policy'.

The two countries are now both strategic and developmental partners with growing multi-vector linkages. Given the far reaching geopolitical and geoeconomic changes taking place in the Indo-Pacific, it should be mentioned that the two countries should intensify collaboration not only in ASEAN but also in the broader context of Indo-Pacific. India and Vietnam have a convergence of views on various regional and international issues. It is now important that this convergence extends to better understanding of each other's perspective and interests in the Indo-Pacific.

High Potential for Cooperation in Defence

Defence cooperation brings extended benefits for India and Vietnam. India has commited to assisting Vietnam in modernizing defence and security forces by training, joint military exercise and developing defence industry, especially for producing light weapons. Accordingly, production of military equipment and coaching instruments is also an area of cooperation being strengthened by India and Vietnam. In recent years, Vietnam has also been upgrading its military equipment along with modernization of national armed forces. This has found favours with the Narendra Modi government which considers modernization of military equipment for the settlement of security challengers. A new initiative termed

"Make in India" is being promoted by Prime Minister Narendra Modi to make defence industry and technology facilities of the country more active. India has signed contracts for sale of weapons, military equipment, technologies and services with Vietnam, so that Vietnam can modernize its armed forces, improve ability to repair and maintain weapons and equipment of air force and navy.

According to the Diplomat, India is expected to export at lot of military equipment to Vietnam, including Varunastra anti-submarine torpedo and BrahMos supersonic cruise missiles. [9] India and Vietnam have purchased military equipment from Russia, thus, cooperation related to parts, serving and training is feasible. Negotiations about BrahMos missile purchase and sale show rapid and practical development of Vietnam-India comprehensive partnership in conformity with desire of India to be a large weapon supplier. However, China has emerged as a large weapon seller that does not allow another Asian country to participate in this market. This is one of the reasons for objection of Beijing against participation of India in Nuclear Supplier Group that can expand nuclear industry of India. [10]

In principle, India has agreed to sell missiles (BrahMos) to Vietnam and has been negotiating. Additionally, India has offered sale of Akash missiles also to Vietnam. Akash missiles have operational range of 25 km. against helicopters and unmanned aerial helicopters. Vietnam has paid "much attention" to re-purchase of Akash missiles and negotiated about technology transfer and production of air defence system. If two countries reach a final agreement, Akash missiles will be used in defence system of Vietnam which would increase its ability to defend against a strong China and deterring China from making pre-emptive attacks due to fear of retaliation on a large scale.

However, developments in defence and security relations between India and Vietnam needs to be considered in view of increase in India's military strength and India's active and consistent intervention in Southeast Asia. Vietnam-India comprehensive strategic partnership also needs to be considered as a result of a gradual development in the relationship for many years.

Based on international, regional and local situations, it is imperative that Vietnam maintains on implementing a foreign policy based on an "independent, self-controlled, peaceful diplomacy, and cooperates, develops, diversifies, multilateralizes external relations, proactively and actively integrates into the world and becomes a reliable partner and responsible member of the international community". With such system of proactive and active foreign viewpoints, policies, targets, missions for international integration, it is sure that India would be keen on being a country playing a key role in foreign policy of Vietnam.

The relationship covers a wide range of issues covering political, defence and security relations; trade and commerce; energy cooperation; science and technology; capacity building; connectivity links; health, education, culture, tourism and people to people exchange; and cooperation in international, regional and sub-regional forums.

It is only with such a multi-pronged approach that we can actualise the Comprehensive Strategic Partnership between the two countries and harness the true potential for greatness of our countries and people. [11]

Vietnam and India have upgraded bilateral relations from strategic partnership to comprehensive strategic partnership and India has become one of the three comprehensive strategic partners of Vietnam besides China and Russia.

New developments in cooperation relationship between Vietnam and India need to be considered to originate from demands and benefits each country possesses to improve standing, strength and make contributions for the development of a secured, peaceful and stable atmosphere in the region. Although India and Vietnam have been making progress in cooperation but it is necessary to consider the Chinese factor also because of its emerging and increasing influences in the region. Recent ambitions of China towards the region necessitate cooperation between India and Vietnam. In order to maintain a peaceful environment and prevent possible conflicts, Vietnam aims to maintain a good relationship with China and India and other countries that can balance power in Southeast Asia and assist Vietnam in taking advantage of economic development opportunities.

Vietnam and India share opinions on international and regional issues that two parties pay attention to, including issues related to the East Sea.

According to the Minister of External Affairs, two parties re-declare cooperation for maintenance of peace, stability, safety, security and freedom regarding marine and aviation in Asia-Pacific and the world; emphasize principles of respect for international laws, dispute settlement by peaceful measures based on international laws, and adherence to 1982 United Nations Convention on the Law of the Sea (UNCLOS).

As coordinator of ASEAN-India relations during 2015-2018 period, Vietnam supported increasing comprehensive cooperation between India and the region and active contributions of India as a strong country in Asia. Vietnam keeps on strengthening relations with India in many aspects in the framework of 'Act East Policy'.

On the occasion of visit of the Minister of Foreign Affairs, Pham Binh Minh to India, the two countries signed an Action Program for implementation of Comprehensive Strategic Partnership for the period 2017-2020 between Vietnam and India.

The Action Program is an important framework for initiating comprehensive cooperation in the field of bilateral relations including politics, defence and security, economy, energy, science, information technology, education, training, research, culture, tourism, people-to-people exchange, law and justice, health care, agriculture, fishery and animal husbandry, finance and credit and cooperation in regional and international forums.

Co-operation at Regional Forums

Vietnam supports strengthening of ties between India and ASEAN. Vietnam is considered as a "key pillar" and an "important bridge" for India in the region. Bridge role of Vietnam was more important when Vietnam was ASEAN Coordinator for India for the period 2015-2018. Vietnam always supports and desires increasing cooperation between India and ASEAN. Vietnam has been assisting India in expanding relations with ASEAN and is willing to help India to fund high-class partners in ASEAN Regional Forum (ARF), and East Asia Summit (EAS). Taking advantage of the coordinating role, Vietnam will also support early participation of India in APEC, proactively participate in connection initiatives regarding economy, science, culture between India and ASEAN member states, actively promote implementation of FTA regarding services and investment between ASEAN and India (officially taking effect from July 2015) and keep on effectively participating in multilateral security and defence cooperation mechanism within the framework of ASEAN (ADMM+).

Vietnam supports India becoming a permanent member of the United Nations Security Council. Vietnam and India emphasize for an urgent necessity to reform the United Nations and expansion of the United Nations Security Council for permanent members and non-permanent members with higher number of members from developing countries. Vietnam assisted the Indian nominee in becoming permanent member of the expanded United Nations Security Council.

Conclusion

Vietnam and India have favourable conditions regarding history—in regional and international context—politics, economy, defence and security, science and technology, culture, education, etc. to further their relations in a more comprehensive and intensive manner. In the context that India's 'Act East Policy' has achieved significant developments in favour of relations with Vietnam and Vietnam was the ASEAN coordinator for India for the period of 2015-2018, this is an important milestone for the two countries regarding history, geography, economy and mutual strategies. This is the time for two countries to promote a comprehensive strategic partnership in a pragmatic way.

In the near future, the two countries need to nurture their relations in an effective manner to take advantage of potential strengths of the two nations.

Endnotes

1. Nguyen Ngoc Ha and Nguyen Thi Mai, "The East Sea in Look East Policy of India", Summary Report of International Scientific Workshop: Vietnam-India: 45 Years of Diplomatic Relationship and 10 Years of Strategic Partnership, 2017, The Publishing House of Political Theory, Hanoi, p. 429.
2. Vietnam Trade Office in India (December 2017), "Vietnam-India Trade Reaches $6.86 Billion in the First 11 Months", available at: http://www.moit.gov.vn/web/guest/tin-chi-tiet/-/chi-tiet/thuong-mai-viet-nam-an-%C4%91o-%C4%91at-6-86-ty-usd-trong-11-thang-%C4%91au-nam-10113-401.html.
3. Exurban India (February 2017), "India's Engagements with CLMV: Gateway to ASEAN Markets", available at: https://www.eximbankindia.in/Assets/Dynamic/PDF/Publication-Resources/ResearchPapers/Hindi/69file.pdf, p. 67.
4. Vietnam Trade Office in India (December 2017), "Vietnam-India Trade Reaches $6.86 Billion in the First 11 Months available at: http://www.moit.gov.vn/web/guest/tin-chi-tiet/-/chi-tiet/thuong-mai-viet-nam-an-%C4%91o-%C4%91at-6-86-ty-usd-trong-11-thang-%C4%91au-nam-10113-401.html.
5. "OVL Gets 2-year Extension for Exploring Vietnamese Oil Block (July 2017), available at: https://timesofindia.indiatimes.com/business/india-business/ovl-gets-2-year-extension-for-exploring-vietnamese-oil-block/articleshow/59512646.cms.
6. "Joint Statement between the Socialist Republic of Vietnam and the Republic of India", September, 2016, available at:

http://dantri.com.vn/xa-hoi/toan-van-tuyen-bo-chung-viet-nam-an-do-20160903201752868.htm.

7. DW (2014), "Opinion: Modi Reshapes India's Foreign Policy", available at: http://www.dw.com/en/opinion-modi-reshapes-indias-foreign-policy/a-18159829.
8. The visit of the Deputy Prime Minister, Minister of Foreign Affairs to India (2017).
9. Shaheli Dash (2016), "Modi's Visit to Vietnam: What's on the Agenda?", available at: https://thediplomat.com/2016/08/modis-visit-to-vietnam-whats-on-the-agenda.
10. R.S. Raja Ram Panda, "India and Vietnam: Joint Ties and Supports for Mutual Benefits", Summary Report of Vietnam-India International Scientific Workshop: 45 years of Diplomatic Relationship and 10 years of Strategic Partnership, Ho Chi Minh National Academy of Politics, Hanoi, March, 2017, p. 52.
11. Interview of Ambassador Harsh Parvathaneni with the Vietnam News Agency, (January 8, 2017), "Vietnam a Key Pillar of India's Act East Policy", available at: http://english.vietnamnet.vn/fms/government/170805/vietnam-a-key-pillar-of-india-s-act-east-policy.html.

References

D.W. (2014), "Opinion: Modi Reshapes India's Foreign Policy", available at: http://www.dw.com/en/opinion-modi-reshapes-indias-foreign-policy/a-18159829.

Exim Bank of India (February 2017), "India's Engagements with CLMV: Gateway to ASEAN Markets", available at: https://www.eximbankindia.in/Assets/Dynamic/PDF/Publication-Resources/ResearchPapers/Hindi/69file.pdf.

"Joint Statement between the Socialist Republic of Vietnam and the Republic of India, September 2016, available at: http://dantri.com.vn/xa-hoi/toan-van-tuyen-bo-chung-viet-nam-an-do-20160903201752868.htm.

Nguyen Ngoc Ha and Nguyen Thi Mai (2017), "The East Sea in Look East policy of India", Summary Report of International Scientific Workshop: Vietnam-India: 45 years of Diplomatic

Relationship and 10 Years of Strategic Partnership, The Publishing House of Political Theory, Hanoi, p. 429.

"OVL Gets 2-year Extension for Exploring Vietnamese Oil Block July 2017, available at: https://timesofindia.indiatimes.com/business/india-business/ovl-gets-2-year-extension-for-exploring-vietnamese-oil-block/articleshow/59512646.cms.

R.S. Rajaram Panda (2017), "India and Vietnam: Joint Ties and Supports for Mutual Benefits", Summary Report of Vietnam-India International Scientific Workshop: 45 years of Diplomatic Relationship and 10 Years of Strategic Partnership, Ho Chi Minh National Academy of Politics, Hanoi, March, p. 52.

Shaheli Das (2016), "Modi's Visit to Vietnam: What's On the Agenda?", available at: https://thediplomat.com/2016/08/modis-visit-to-vietnam-whats-on-the-agenda.

Vietnam Net Bridge (2017), "Vietnam, India to Co-operate on Maritime Matters", available at: http://english.vietnamnet.vn/fms/government/187245/vietnam--india-to-co-operate-on-maritime-matters.html.

7

China in Maldives: India's Concerns

Gayathry Gopal

Maldives, a member of SAARC, is a micro state consisting of a chain of 1,192 islands and 26 atolls. Located at the centre of Gulf of Aden and Strait of Malacca, the island nation is of immense strategic importance. With its small size and narrow resource base, it is relatively proximate to its bigger neighbours and is increasingly dependent on outside powers. The political framework of Maldives is that of a presidential representative democratic republic. Since its transition to democracy, Maldives has been witness to a number of domestic instabilities. This includes threats to the democratisation process in Maldives during Abdulla Yemen's regime which became increasingly autocratic. Another pressing challenge for this Indian Ocean littoral state is the increasing radicalization of what has been a moderate society. Adding to the miseries of the island nation is the issue of climate change. Coupled with the domestic challenges is an economy troubled with increasing foreign debts and external dependence.

The rise of China and India has increased the geopolitical significance of the Indian Ocean region. The changing geopolitics of the region has conferred immense strategic importance to the littoral. Maldives has undoubtedly turned sensitive geopolitically due to the presence of competing global and regional powers. Take the case of India; Maldives is just 300 miles away from its Southern Cost. Being an important member of SAARC and with its location in the major sea lanes of Indian Ocean, Maldives is of critical strategic and geopolitical importance to India. On the other hand is China, an emerging global power, which has given up its quite diplomacy and has become increasingly assertive. China is more than ever active in South Asia economically and politically. Beijing with ambitious projects like OBOR (One Belt One Road Initiative) is aiming at strategic supremacy in the Indian Ocean Region.

Of late, India has also made explicit its goals of becoming a 'leading power' than a balancing power. India's grooming of its geopolitical ambitions takes the form of expansion of security ties with littoral states, regional and global powers, construction of military bases, modernized equipment and fleets and increased multilateral naval ties with the countries in the IOR. During the 1960s, India opposed the involvement of big powers in the Indian Ocean region. There is marked change in this attitude. India has over the years been actively engaging major powers like U.S.A, Japan etc. in the Indian Ocean Region. India does not want to lose its grip in a region which is crucial in terms of security as well as supply lines. Given this context, this paper analyses India-Maldives relationship amidst China's growing influence in the island nation.

Regional groupings rising to prominence has been a marked feature of the post-Cold War era. Successful regional groupings in Europe and North America have encouraged such arrangements in other parts of the world as well. Going with the trend, India too has become an active participant in many regional arrangements across South Asia and Southeast Asia. India primarily aims at enhancing multilateral cooperation and boosting the stability of the region. In the context of South Asia, its main regional organization, SAARC unfortunately has failed to deliver the goal of regional integration. 'Dealing it bilaterally' is still the South Asian way. For India to secure its interests, it is left with the only option of dealing with its smaller neighbours bilaterally. This is exactly why New Delhi is concerned when other powers step into what has been traditionally considered as its sphere of influence.

Evolution of a Genuine Bilateral Relation

A 'friend in need'—this is what India has been to Maldives all these years. India's cultural, religious, linguistic, ethnic and commercial links with the island nation has a history that can be traced since antiquity. Freedom from British came in the year 1966 for Maldives and India was one of the first nations to recognize the Independence of Maldives. A bilateral treaty signed on August 8, 1949 provides the framework of India-Maldives relations. The principle of beneficial bilateralism guides the bilateral relations among the two. Mutual appreciation of issues and concerns and equal respect and understanding of each other's sensitivities has strengthened this relationship over the years (Chakrabarthy, Chandramohan).

Maldives-India relation was mostly free of the issues that usually confront the relation between a small nation and a big power as the relationship was based on mutual understanding, respect and a genuine desire for cooperation. India had its resident high commissioner in Male since 1980. A full-fledged High Commission was opened in New Delhi by Maldives in November 2004. Frequent high level visits have nurtured the bilateral relationship over the years. The mutual understanding between the two nations is appreciable and was evident in the way the two countries demarcated their maritime boundary in 1976 using the median principle.

India and Maldives signed a comprehensive trade agreement in 1981. A milestone in the relation between two countries came when India stepped in to rescue Maldives from a coup by the militants of People's Liberation Organisation of Tamil Eelam (a Tamil secessionist organization from Sri Lanka) headed by Abdullah Luthafi. The militants took control of the airport in Male. Indian forces arrived within hours after the request for aid from Male and launched 'Operation Cactus'. India's intervention was appreciated and has been considered as a valuable contribution to regional security. India also maintains a naval presence in the island nation since

2009 as per its request. India was the first to provide Maldives with relief supplies after the Tsunami of December 26, 2004.

In 2014, India also dispatched water aid when a major damage occurred at Maldives's biggest water treatment plant. Thus, the history of relation between both nations is one of close cooperation.

Areas of Cooperation

India and Maldives, over the years, have expanded the areas of cooperation. Culture is one of the foremost important factors that bring the two countries together. Indian cultural centre was established in the island nation in July 2011. Close political relationship is maintained through regular contacts at the highest level. Since the establishment of diplomatic relations between the two countries, the heads of states had paid regular visits. The first democratically elected president of Maldives, Mohammed Nasheed, chose India as the destination for his first foreign visit. High level visits are also held regularly at the ministerial level.

An important area of cooperation between the two countries is defence. Two countries have been conducting a series of coast guard maritime training exercise codenamed 'Dosti' since 1991. Ekuverin, a joint army training exercise, is conducted between the countries aiming at enhancing the military ties. Also, a large number of defence service personnel from Maldives are trained in various defence establishments in India. On April 2006, Indian navy gifted a fast track aircraft to the National Defence Force's Coast Guard of Maldives. India and Maldives signed the defence pact in 2009. According to the pact, active operation assistance by India's tri-services will be provided to the Maldivian armed forces. Intelligence sharing is another important area coming under the pact. India has also set up a radar network which will be linked to the Indian surveillance systems. Maritime surveillance will thus safeguard Maldives's strategic maritime assets. The defence pact also includes the protection of Maldivian exclusive economic zone.

Another vital part of this multidimensional relation is economic cooperation. Indian export to Maldives mainly consists of agriculture and poultry produce. Sugar, fruits, vegetables, spices and rice are the main items of export. Maldives mainly exports scrap metals to India. As per the bilateral agreement, essential food items are provided to Maldives on favourable terms. Extensive economic aid is being provided by India to Maldives. There are also many assistance programmes aimed at development of infrastructure, civil aviation, health care etc. State Bank of India has provided about US$ 500 million aiming at the economic expansion of Maldives.

Human resource development is another area where two countries have been cooperating. India provides both long-term and short-term training under various schemes. Areas covered include social sciences, commerce, IT and medicine.

Close cooperation also exists between two countries in the area of maritime search and rescue, humanitarian assistance and disaster relief, marine pollution response, anti-piracy operation and disaster management. Capacity building and training are also part of this multi-dimensional relationship. In the international area too, both countries have served as a constant source of support to each other. They have often supported each other's candidature to various international bodies.

Major Concerns for India

The state of Maldives is confronting issues like political instability, economic dependence, increasing radicalisation, waning democracy and adverse climatic conditions. These internal problems influence the foreign policy decisions as well. The political crisis began after the first democratic elections mainly due to the difference in opinion between political parties. Mohammed Nasheed, the first democratically elected president, was forced to resign. In the second parliamentary elections in 2014, a new coalition government came to power. By 2015, the country was experiencing greater centralization of power in the country. The opposition leaders were arrested; repeated interference of the Supreme Court in the elections and frequent constitutional amendments further weakened the democracy. Since 2008, India has been very cautious about its response regarding the internal issues of Maldives.

When Mr. Nasheed took refuge in Indian embassy to evade his arrest, Indian officials decided to broker a peace deal. When Nasheed was arrested, India expressed its concern over the developments. India being cautious about taking a strong position shows New Delhi's wish to avoid a strain in the relationship between the two nations.

Maldives's strategic location makes it vulnerable since outside powers are eyeing for strategic advantage. What aggravates this vulnerability is the absence of adequate military strength to ensure its own safety.

Following the rejection of India's appeal regarding Mr. Nasheed, Prime Minister Narendra Modi had to drop Maldives from his four Nation Indian Ocean tour in 2015. Thus, India was making evident its disappointments with the developments. Apart from the domestic political instabilities, India is increasingly concerned about the rising radicalisation of Maldivian society. In 2014, a group of people marched in Male waving black flags of the Islamic State (IS). Poverty and deprivation among certain communities can be cited as one of the reasons behind radicalisation. Ease of raising funds through money laundering is also helping the growth of terrorist groups.

China is making inroads into every South Asian country by virtue of its growing economy. Maldives is no exception to this. India often accuses China of encirclement. All countries except India and Bhutan have joined China's One Belt One Road initiative. Sino-Maldives relations have grown remarkably since the visit of Chinese President Xi Jinping in

September 2014. There were strains in India-Maldives relation ever since China has asserted its presence in the island nation. Some of the major irritants in the relation include Male's termination of the agreement it signed with GMR in 2010 for the modernization of Ibrahim Nasir International Airport. GMR said the termination was unlawful and irrational. A high voltage legal battle followed the termination. The project that was taken away from GMR has now been granted to a state-owned Chinese company.

Maldives in 2015 amended its Constitution to allow foreign nationals to buy land on any of the islands. Previously, foreign ownership of any part of Maldivian territory was prohibited. The current amendment allows land to be leased for a period of 99 years. The speed at which the amendment was passed is also of much concern to India. The amendment could pave way for increased Chinese naval presence in the region. China is involved in the creation of artificial islands in South China Sea. Some Indian officials have expressed their concern about a Chinese attempt at trying something similar in this region as well. Though China has dismissed all such concerns, there are indications that People's Liberation Army-Navy (PLAN) aims at enhancing its capabilities for strategic deterrence and counter-attack, maritime manoeuvres, joint operations at sea etc. Chinese naval presence in Pakistan's Gwadar port is adding strength to India's doubts (Haan).

China's presence in the Maldives tourist sector has expanded. Earlier, Europe was the largest source of tourism and now this position has been taken over by China. By increasing the number of direct flights from Maldives to mainland China, Beijing has ensured an increase in the inflow of tourists to Maldives. Infrastructure building is another area where China's overwhelming presence can be seen. It is funding many mega infrastructure projects also like the Friendship Bridge linking Male to Hulhule Island. China has granted loans and aid for the Ihavandhippolhu Integrated Development Project also.

The signing of free trade agreement between China and Maldives marks Beijing's success in its outreach in the island nation. Under the FTA, China and Maldives would be reducing the tariffs of more than 95 percent of the goods to zero. The agreement also aims at opening the service market such as finance, tourism and healthcare. The way the FTA was rushed through the parliament in a midnight session has received sharp criticism from inside and has send alarming signals to New Delhi. The free trade agreement will increase the Chinese role in the Maldivian economy.

Energy and geostrategic imperatives are driving Chinese activities in the Indian Ocean region. Indian strategists talk about the Chinese string of pearls that aims at raising military infrastructure on chosen spots in IOR. These chosen points are islands or ports in specific areas like Strait of Malacca, Sri Lanka, Pakistan, Maldives, and Strait of Hormuz etc. This can have adverse strategic implications for India in its own backyard. Recently, Maldives has leased an island close to Male Airport to China. In August 2017, Maldives permitted three Chinese warships to dock in Male.

It is true that under the regime of President Abdulla Yameen, the island nation was drawn close to China. This pro-China policy has forced India to question Yameen's self-proclaimed 'India First Policy'. India is also aware of an impending debt trap that might hit the island nation.

A Rising China

Gerald Segalin (1999) asked the question 'Does China Matter'? The question is no longer relevant as China is now a global power. The rise of China is increasingly changing the geopolitics of South Asia. China maintained its economic growth momentum despite the global financial crisis. This has helped China in increasing its trade and commercial links with the South Asian Countries. The uncertainty in the US position is also encouraging China to be more active in the region. China is already replacing the US-led institutions in infrastructure development programmes. China has also launched the ambitious One Belt One Road Initiative (OBOR) with the end goal of mastery over oceans and connectivity routes. Many view it as a political project and its economic viability being secondary.

Different schools of thought have come up with their version of dealing with the rise of China. Some talk about it from a revisionist perspective. Yet, China cannot be called revisionist as such, though some of the activities of China shows a revisionist orientation. The writer here is of the view that realist theory could better explain the Chinese behaviour. Yet, there exists a debate amongst the realist school regarding which strand of realism would suit the case. The answer is realism should return to some of its classical traditions. A classical realist approach allows for the influence of history and politics and has greater analytical purpose and wiser policy prescriptions than other strands of realism, say for example offensive realism.

Waltz' version of realism has been a paradigm shift that has provided a breakthrough from the classical prism of the primacy of the 'state' to the broader unit of the 'international' or the 'system'. But it overemphasizes on the systemic level of analysis. Asian region in general is state-centred and emphasizes on the traditional norms of state sovereignty. Offensive realists argue that states are motivated to secure their own survival and will recognize regional hegemony as the safest position in the international system. Classical realists like George F. Kennan are of the view that no people are great enough to establish global hegemony (Karishner).

The major problem here is that if survival was its main goal then only a power completely ignorant of history will embark upon a bid for hegemony! Karishner says, "classical realists would expect states to understand that throwing their weight around in a bid for hegemony might be a self-defeating exercise, whereas structural realists will make the same foolish choices over and over again" (Karishner).

John Mearsheimer, talks about the success story of U.S. But he forgets to mention that there were other powers that fought wars for regional hegemony—imperial Japan, Wilhelmine Germany, Napoleonic France, and Nazi Germany—where none succeeded. If the US succeeded, it was mainly due to two factors, that is, 'weak neighbours' and 'weak adversaries'. But this is not the case with China. Hence, an offensive realist idea may not be helpful. Classical realist strategy of dealing with the Chinese phenomena is to engage it rather than confronting it. Two positions that classical realists can seek to pursue in a broader framework of engagement with China include the need to acknowledge power; both the reality of the power of others and the necessary limitations of one's own. The idea of accommodation is central in classical realist thought. Another important factor is that politics matters: both domestic and international. That is, choices made by states are affected by what goes on inside of them, and choices made by states are also affected by choices made by other states. Classical realism also places great emphasis on politics, domestic and international, and even considers the role of things like ideas, norms, and legitimacy (Karishner).

Indian Ocean: A Region of Competition

The strains that appeared in the India-Maldives relation and the rising influence of China should be seen in a larger context of two Asian giants competing for the control of the strategically important Indian Ocean Region. China has already emerged as a global power. Of late, India too has made explicit its goals of becoming a leading power than a balancing power. The shift from 'Look East Policy' to 'Act East Policy' and reinforcement of its regional maritime presence are all part of New Delhi's push to assert itself as a big power. Its power goals has led to the expansion of security ties, construction of military bases, modernized equipment and fleets and increased multilateral naval ties. China's international influence and greater economic capability will be a great challenge especially when there is a clash of interests between the two countries.

The Indian Ocean Region is responsible for two-thirds of world's oil shipment and one-third of world cargo movement. Approximately, eighty percent of India's energy imports are through this region. Hence, it has always remained its top priority. During the 1960s, India's policy was that of keeping the major powers out of the Indian Ocean Region. In the 1990s, India opened up its economy and welcomed globalization. This also ended its military isolation. India's UPA government was enthusiastic about its activities in the region. It tried bringing dynamism in the Indian Ocean Rim Association. It also organized the Indian Ocean Naval Symposium which included the naval chiefs of littoral states and provided a platform to promote maritime security and professional exchanges. India in 2011 initiated a trilateral security arrangement involving Sri Lanka and Maldives to expand maritime security cooperation.

The policies embarked upon by the Indian government in the recent years reveal that Indian Ocean is at New Delhi's top priorities. It is also aware of the growing strategic significance of the region in international politics. India is now willing to do whatever that is necessary to protect its mainland as well as island territories. For this, India is focusing on deepening security cooperation with its regional allies. India also aims at sustainable economic development in the region. This implies taking into consideration the ecology while harnessing the resources. India also aims at multilateral cooperation for maritime security and for this it has discarded its previous reluctance to involve other major powers in the region.

Both China and India insist on exerting influence by involving themselves in port developments in littoral states and military patrols. Through launching counter piracy operations, Beijing has been increasingly active in the region. India is also reinforcing its regional maritime presence. India has increased its expenditure in naval build up. India initiated a bilateral naval exercise with Australia also. It also participated in multi-lateral naval games with US, Japan and Australia. In spite of this, China is expanding its foothold in the region. It is increasingly involved in infrastructure development activities. This also includes Chinese naval presence in strategic locations in states like Maldives and Sri Lanka. The OBOR initiative aims at strategic supremacy in the Indian Ocean Region. India refused to participate in the Belt and Road Initiative Project forum which was held in May 2017.

India stressed that connectivity cannot undermine the sovereignty of other nations. But with all countries in the South Asian Region expect Bhutan joining the OBOR initiative, India fears containment at its own backyard. With the progress of China-Pakistan Economic Corridor through the territory that is claimed by India, it suspects new pathways of aggression being created. Indian experts are worried about the long-term strategic consequence of OBOR. OBOR might help China consolidate its position in the Indian Ocean at the expense of India. China might also use its economic power to increase its geopolitical leverage. This might intensify security concerns for India.

India Acting East

India has recently opted for a transition from 'Look East' to 'Act East' policy. 'Act East Policy' focuses on its neighbourhood in the Asia-Pacific region. The objective of the policy is to promote economic cooperation, and developing strategic relationship and cultural ties with the countries in the region. Indo-Pacific region is important when the global economy and global geopolitics is considered. China is making good fortune out of an unstable US stand in the region. This is what makes this transition period important for countries like India. With US being unsure of its security commitments and a growing Chinese presence, the region provides India with new opportunities.

'Act East Policy' is not driven by a single goal, but by many. One is definitely to counterbalance the rise of Chinese regional influence. Secondly, it aims at increasing Indian services and goods exports. India also looks forward for the development of the country's North-Eastern part through infrastructure projects linking India with its bordering South East Asian countries and beyond. Following the balance of payment crisis of 1991, India began opening itself up to the world. It was during this transition period, the then Prime Minister Narasimha Rao decided to look east toward the fast-growing economies of the Association of Southeast Asian Nations (ASEAN). His 'Look East Policy' was a conscious effort aimed at reorienting Indian trade towards Asia.

The present NDA government under Narendra Modi is determined to elevate India's global profile and economic diplomacy being the key element of Modi's foreign policy. It tries to promote economic growth by inviting greater foreign investment and expanding trade. The government also wants to increase its defence budget to spend more on its navy to enhance its ability to project power more effectively. It is with these aims in mind, Modi announced the up gradation from 'Look East' to 'Act East' in the East Asia Summit in November.

Though trade is important, one distinguishing feature of the 'Act East Policy' is its emphasis on an enhanced regional security role for India both within and beyond the ASEAN states. It is clear that India wants to keep China's regional maritime ambitions in check. It is said that the common aim of counterbalancing China is bringing India, Japan and the United States towards closer military cooperation. Also India and Japan are boosting their bilateral relations through cooperation on counterterrorism and joint military exercises. Most importantly, Japan and India is looking forward to develop the Asia-Africa Growth Corridor which is viewed as an answer to China's Belt and Road Initiative.

India's activities in this region are driven mainly by self-interest. New Delhi's strategy includes imposing secondary costs on China on the maritime front. Both India and Southeast Asian nations wish to promote open seas and freedom for navigation. India has already strengthened its naval ties with countries such as Singapore, Vietnam, Thailand, Malaysia and Indonesia. Also many of the land-locked countries in the region expect greater involvement of India in the region. Indian officials have expressed the view that China's hegemonic moves in the South China Sea in the past few years have made ASEAN countries to look towards India for maintaining the equilibrium.

Current Political Situation in Maldives

The politically turbulent situation that prevailed before the 2018 presidential election has now changed. Before 2018, things took a very ugly turn when the Supreme Court of the country gave the verdict to release political prisoners and reinstate the members of Parliament who have been removed by President Yameen. The top court also threw out the case against former President Mohammed Nasheed. The then government under Abdulla Yameen responded by arresting the top two judges who delivered the verdict and declared an emergency for 15 days. This poured in criticism from both inside and outside the country. India, along with US, UK, and the United Nations condemned the emergency. India even issued a warning to its citizens to avoid all non-essential travel to the island nation.

When Abdulla Yameen started consolidating his power, the opposition groups in Maldives were desperately requesting for intervention from outside. They were explicit in their request to India to intervene militarily. First, democratically elected President Nasheed too has made the same request and called India the 'Liberator' of the Island Nation. China was quick in its response and had warned against all kinds of outside intervention. Beijing called on the international community to respect the sovereignty of Maldives and to avoid any kind of actions that may further complicate the situation. Chinese media was critical of India's position. An article on People's daily website hinted of 'an invisible hand' influencing the events in Maldives. Global Times said India has 'no rights' to meddle with the sovereignty of Maldives. The Maldivian government too was sharp in its reaction. It warned against the calls for military intervention to resolve the crisis and asserted that it firmly believes that India would not react on any such calls.

Though India was deeply concerned about the events that happened in Maldives, it clearly refused to undertake military action of any kind. Rather it chose to act diplomatically, respecting the sovereignty of its neighbour. India along with other countries succeeded in putting tremendous pressure on Yameen's government to conduct the Presidential elections in a transparent manner.

In what has been a peaceful and democratic election, people of Maldives gave their verdict and in September 2018, Ibrahim Mohamed Solih took charge as the new President.

Aiming at a Sustainable Relationship

Any instability in the region and hegemony of any one power can be adverse and it needs to be avoided. Despite the fact that South Asia is Indo-centric in terms of geography, culture, economy and infrastructure, India has not succeeded in establishing itself as a regional power. The very cultural, religious and geographical factors that connects India with its neighbours, also alienates it from them. With China forging closer links with every nation in South Asia, New Delhi fears isolation and containment. India is no more passive in responding to China's assertiveness. India has reinforced its regional maritime presence. It is also involving other major powers like US and Japan to counter China. But unreliability of the partnership with US is a setback to India.

Though the 'Act East Policy' is being hailed as India's response to Chinese engagement in South Asian region, its implementation needs to deal with numerous hurdles. The hurdles include issues of protectionism, inability of the ASEAN economies to afford India's high-value IT exports and India's reluctance to get involved in South China Sea dispute etc.

Now coming to the case of Maldives, the stands of present government of Maldives are definitely a change from the autocratic stand of Yameen. Solih's regime saw the island nation reconnecting with many countries particularly India. New Delhi was also quick in befriending the new ruling party. Prime Minister Narendra Modi was present in the swearing ceremony of Mr Solih. Solih in his maiden visit to India reiterated 'India-First Policy'. He has also acknowledged the assistance given by India to Maldives.

President Solih was open in his criticism of Yameen that he was playing China against India and vice-versa. Though Solih has not completely unfriended China, he said he will revise the controversial FTA signed with China during Yameen's presidency.

India cannot or should not expect a complete revision in Maldives attitude to China. China, given the economic opportunities it is capable of providing, will remain a priority for Maldives. Though the current high level visits and India's offer of $1.4 billion as assistance suggest a positive turn and renewed enthusiasm in the relationship between the two, the idea is to foster a long-term sustainable relationship.

Even if we are talking from the perspective of Male, what it should aim is a sustainable economic growth. The World Bank has warned Male about the debt trap. Maldives owes more than 70 percent of its debt to one country that is China. A debt trap might push Maldives into Chinese security net. The exploitation of land ownership rights might be detrimental to the sovereignty of the island nation. Male should be careful while lavishly leasing its land to foreign countries. It won't be too good for Maldives to completely ignore its immediate neighbour who has proved to be a genuine friend in the past.

India should reinvigorate the policy of 'beneficial bilateralism' that has been guiding the relationship between India and Maldives in the past. It is particularly important because, the idea of accommodating each other's sensitivities is implicit in this policy.

Regarding China, it would be unwise for New Delhi to ignore the disparities in the relative spending capacities. With its project management skills and huge influx of infrastructural investment, China is at an advantageous position in comparison to India. Yet the idea of outright containment of China would result in a zero sum game. The US centric strategy of balancing China may not prove fruitful given the unsurely commitment of Washington regarding this region. A direct confrontation can be counterproductive. Hence, India should look forward to 'engage' China rather than 'confronting' China. Engaging China through multi-lateral cooperation on issues like terrorism, climate change, anti-piracy activities etc. would be more fruitful and sustainable in the long-run.

References

Albert, Eleanor, Council on Foreign Relations, May 19, 2016, available at:
https://www.cfr.org/backgrounder/competition-indian-ocean.

Chakrabarthy, Manas, et al. (2016), "India-Maldives: A Study of Bilateral Relationship", *FRPC Journal*, 2277-2464.

Darling, Daniel, "Real Clear Defense", November 3, 2016, available at:
https://www.realcleardefense.com/articles/2016/11/04/the_indian_ocean_emerging_great_power_competition_110308.html.

F., Jean-Marc and Colin Flint (2017), "The Geopolitics of China's Maritime Silk Road Initiative", *Geopolitics*, 223-245.

Gaens, Bart and Olli Rlohomaki, Finnish Institute of International Affairs, May 6, 2017, available at:
https://www.fiia.fi/en/publication/indias-look-east-act-east-policy?read.

Gupta, Aravind, Institute for Defense Studies and Analysis, January 3, 2014, available at: https://idsa.in/policybrief/IndiaandMaldives_agupta_130113.

Haan, Jarryd de, Future Directions International, July 29, 2015, available at: http://www.futuredirections.org.au/publication/maldives-constitutional-amendment-makes-a-chinese-port-possible.

Hudda, Nabit, International Relations, April 3, 2015, available at: http://www.e-ir.info/2015/04/03/interpreting-the-rise-of-china-realist-and-liberalist-perspectives.

Karishner, Jonathan (2010), "The Tragedy of Offensive Realism: Classical Realism and the Rise of China", *European Journal of International Relations*.

Krishnan, Anantha, India Today, January 24, 2018, available at: https://www.indiatoday.in/magazine/up-front/story/20171120-east-asia-india-asean-summit-act-east-policy-pm-modi-1082494-2017-11-10.

Mohan, C. Raja, The National Interest, June 26, 2016, available at: http://nationalinterest.org/blog/the-buzz/revealed-indias-master-plan-the-indian-ocean-13198.

Manoharan, N., Institute of Peace and Conflict Studies, June 28, 2017, available at: http://www.ipcs.org/article/india/india-maldives-relations-a-tale-of-two-concerns-5311.html.

Pant, Harsh V., Yale Global Online, June 22, 2017, available at: https://yaleglobal.yale.edu/content/india-challenges-chinas-intentions-one-belt-one-road-initiative.

Ramachandran, Sudha, The Diplomat, January 25, 2018, available at: https://thediplomat.com/2018/01/the-china-maldives-connection.

Startford Worldview, November 10, 2017, available at: https://worldview.stratfor.com/article/counter-china-india-pushes-east.

Vijay, Sakhuja, Institute of Peace and Conflict Studies, March 3, 2014, available at: http://www.ipcs.org/staff_details.php?member_id=253.

8

Seeking Partnership with Taiwan: India's Big Power Ambitions

Suresh K.

Despite the changes in the nomenclature, one of the basic objectives of India's foreign policy over the years is to find a rightful place among the comity of nations. Strategies like non-alignment or mixed economy, during the early years of Independence can be viewed as a strategy to maintain its autonomy in foreign policy decisions. The basic objective of 'Look East Policy' and the 'Act East Policy' also more or less remained the same. It seeks to revitalize India's economic contact with Southeast Asian States.

Subsequently, besides economic interest, various securities and strategic aspects were added to it. In the post-Cold War milieu, India due to its increased power, both in the economic and strategic field, decided to play an important role in international affairs. It formed alliances with states that are not being unattended. Among the East Asian states, Taiwan is one state which has been given importance in India's 'Act East Policy'. This is mainly due to the shared concerns of both India and Taiwan in multiple areas like economic, cultural and strategic areas. In this paper, an attempt has been made to evaluate the strategic significance of Taiwan in India's 'Act East Policy' and how it influences India's big power ambitions in the future.

One of the basic objectives of India's foreign policy over the years is to find a rightful place among the comity of nations. Right from the very beginning, after Independence, India opted strategies like non-alignment and mixed economy with the basic objective of keeping away from bloc politics and thereby moulding an independent foreign policy for socio-economic development. As such, India's relations with countries in Southeast Asia and East Asia remained minimal for a long period of time. It was only during the 1990s, things began to change. This mutual disengagement, which continued during the Cold War period, was the result of so many factors. First, the countries in the region were in the US camp and are deeply concerned with the spread of communism. Due to their allegiance to United States, India distrusted ASEAN and considered it as a US construct. ASEAN, on the other hand, considered India's soft policy towards USSR as a tilt in its non-alignment policy.

Therefore, both India and Asian countries did not trust each other. Second, the gap between the material and ideological pursuit of the post-independent elites in India also increased the detachment between India and Southeast Asian countries. The post-independent elites in India, due to their liberal ideology and social and educational ties associated themselves with the West. But their ideological commitment to oppose colonialism and the choice of a planned economy placed them at the socialist camp. Thus, the post-independent elites considered East Asia as less attractive. Finally, India and East Asia were never neighbours in the true sense. The lack of adequate physical connectivity secluded them for a long period of time (Singh, 2014).

The changed international conditions after the end of Cold War compelled India to reorient its foreign policy objectives and strategies to meet the challenges and opportunities offered by the new order. The inauguration of 'Look East Policy' by P.V. Narasimha Rao in 1990s was one such change. The basic objective of 'Look East Policy' was to revitalize India's contact with Southeast Asian states after a long period of European colonialism. As a result, relations with countries like Japan, Korea, Malaysia, Singapore, Thailand etc. increased substantially. Subsequently, besides economic interest, various securities and strategic aspects were added to it. When the 'Act East Policy' was inaugurated in 2014, it sought to revitalize India's engagement with not only Southeast Asian states but also to the extended neighbourhood states in the Asia-Pacific region.

However, a close examination of India's foreign policy over the years shows that there are certain areas where Indian foreign policy had given little attention. Among the East Asian states, Taiwan is one state which has been given little importance. A significant change, though very small in number, occurred as a result of 'Look East Policy' and subsequently in 'Act East Policy' as well. This is mainly due to the shared concerns of both India and Taiwan in multiple areas including economic, cultural, and strategic.

Taiwan and the World Politics

There are increasing concerns over the role of Taiwan in India's foreign policy. This is mainly based on the foreign policy calculations i.e. the cost-benefit calculations or the comparative advantage of both countries in terms of their geography, population, size, legal status etc. Therefore, any discussion on Taiwan should begin with its space in international system. Taiwan is a small country in terms of its geography i.e. the territory of Taiwan is 35,980 square kilometres, a size similar to the size of Kerala or 90 times smaller than India. The population of Taiwan is 23 million, similar to the population of Australia or Haryana state or 52 times smaller than India.

Although Taiwan is fully self-sovereign, most international organizations in which Peoples Republic of China participates, either refuses to grant membership to Taiwan or allow it to participate only as a non-state actor. As of today, only 22 small Central American, African, and Pacific Countries recognize the ROC diplomatically (Singh, 2016). The rest of the states maintain unofficial ties through representative offices and institutions that function as de facto embassies and consulates. But at the same time, this should not undermine Taiwan's positive features also. Taiwan is the 22nd largest country in terms of economy. It is from many perspectives virtually a middle power, with a population greater than about three-quarters of the world's countries, a substantial military, an advanced economy and foreign exchange reserves larger than those of India (Jacob, 2016). Its high-tech industry also plays a key role in global economy.

India and Taiwan in Historical Perspective

Until 1949, there were friendly relations between India and Taiwan. Before independence, Chiang Kai-Shek, the political and military leader of the Republic of China (ROC) visited India in 1942 and held discussions with the Indian Prime Minister Jawaharlal Nehru about the future of India as well as Asia. He also supported Indian independence movement and sent an ambassador to India in 1947. All these initiatives, done at the cost of its relations with Britain, did not receive the same warmth from India. From 1949 onwards, India did not maintain any kind of institutionalized contact with Republic of China. The official recognition of People's Republic of China and One China Policy by India naturally increased the distance between the two countries. Throughout the Cold War period both states placed themselves at the opposite poles.

India joined the non-alignment movement and Taiwan joined the US led coalition. However, in the late 1990s, relations between the two countries began to improve. The inauguration of 'Look East Policy' by Narasimha Rao government has brought about such a change. Subsequently in 1995, both the countries set up offices in their respective capital cities. The India-Taipei association (ITA) in Taiwan and The Taipei Economic and Cultural Centre (TECC) in India was established which provided future direction for the relations between the two countries. Even though they were non-official organizations, they worked as official channels of communication to promote the working relations between India and Taiwan on every front (Pande, 2016).

Thereafter, India-Taiwan relations have progressed considerably despite having any diplomatic sanctions to their ties. In 2002, the directors of ITA and TECC signed an agreement for the promotion and protection of investment. The two countries also signed the Double Taxation Avoidance Agreement and the Customs Cooperation agreement in 2011. Direct airstrips started between the two capitals in 2003. In 2007, the ITA and the TECC signed a MoU on behalf of the India's Department of Science and Technology under the Ministry of Science and Technology and Taiwan's NSC. There is also considerable increase in the growth of trade and investment, economic contacts, political engagements and increasing educational linkages between India and Taiwan.

In 2014, when Narendra Modi became the PM of India, there was a renewed attempt to upgrade the relations between the two countries. His victory was welcomed by Taiwan as an opportunity to further upgrade the relations. The Deputy Minister of Economic Affairs of Taiwan was invited to attend the Vibrant Gujarat Conference in 2015. Modi was one of the few Indian politicians to visit Taiwan in 1999, as the General Secretary of BJP and he also hosted the largest-ever Taiwanese business delegation in India as the Chief Minister of Gujarat in 2011 (Sandano, 2017). Moreover, the 'Look East Policy' was refined as 'Act East Policy' to give more emphasis on the relations between East Asian states.

But at the same time, the scale and intensity of the bilateral relations between India and Taiwan have been so slow that it does not demonstrate any effective application of 'Look East' or 'Act East Policy' (Singh, 2016). Comparing India's relations with China, Japan and South Korea, with those of Taiwan, it is very spectacular that Taiwan is off the radar of India's 'Look East' or 'Act East Policy'. It is also noted that if most other countries in East Asia, including those immediately neighbouring China, have robust economic ties with Taiwan as well as significant people-to-people movements and interactions, it is a wonder why India with its difficult relationship with China does not/did not interact more closely with Taiwan at multiple levels (Jacob, 2016).

Bilateral Cooperation

There are so many areas where India and Taiwan can cooperate for mutual progress and development. They have complimentary economies, shared concerns over their security interests, cultural affinities etc. India-Taiwan relations have two dimensions: bilateral relations for regional strategic security and bilateral relations for mutual economic development.

Strategic Relations

India and Taiwan share similar values and there are no serious disputes between the two countries. The emergence of China as a major actor in East Asia and its increasing assertiveness has offered both opportunities and challenges. China has a very decisive role in determining the future course of relations between India and Taiwan. At the strategic security level, both India and Taiwan share similar security interests and concerns. Both the countries have similar security threats and territorial disputes with China. For Taiwan, despite its confirmation to One China Policy, the number of missiles targeted against Taiwan has gone up to 1,500. Although, Beijing says it would prefer peaceful unification, it asserts its resolve to use force if necessary and codified that resolve in the Anti-Secession Law of 2005 (Bush, 2016). Besides these attempts, China has also used all opportunities to block Taiwan's participation in international space and international organisations.

For India, there are unresolved territorial disputes with China which still continue to exist. Most of these territorial disputes occur when there are high level visits to India. The 2013 confrontation by PLA and Indian troops along the Line of Actual Control, the border standoff at Ladakh in 2014, the Dokhlam standoff in 2017 etc. are instances when there was a direct confrontation between India and China along the borders. China has also increased its sphere of influence in India's immediate neighbours like Pakistan, Sri Lanka, Bangladesh, Maldives etc. Since India and Taiwan remain conscious and watchful of the implications of China's increasing military profile in the neighbourhood, there is much common ground on how to deal with shared concerns (Fang, 2015). Thus, China factor has brought both India and Taiwan to closer defence and security cooperation.

Besides these, the emerging common area of strategic partnership between India and Taiwan is on the recently emerging Indo-Pacific construct. Indo-Pacific is a geographical combination of Indian Ocean and the Pacific Ocean that link energy security and maritime security with regional security. Indo-Pacific has become an area of strategic competition by major powers like US, India, China, Japan and Australia. The US policy of Asian rebalancing, China's Maritime Silk Road and India's 'Act East Policy' converge on the Indo-Pacific region. Major economies in East Asia are heavily dependent on crude oil, natural gas and raw materials shipped from the Middle East and Africa through the Indian Ocean and the Pacific Ocean.

Therefore, the Sea Lanes of Communications (SLOCs) from Indian Ocean to the Pacific Ocean have become critical to the strategic interest of East Asian states (Liu, 2016). As the East Asian economies grow fast, their dependence upon energy supply from the Middle East and Africa become critical for their sustained development. They also export industrial products to African countries, Middle East and Europe through the Indian Ocean. All states in East Asia have therefore, a very significant stake in the Indo-Pacific region.

As an energy scarce state, China is increasingly dependent on Indo-Pacific region for the shipment of energy resources from the Middle East and Africa. About 85 percent of oil imported by China passes through the *Strait of Malacca* (Liu, 2016). In order to protect this energy supply, China is driven to set up its military presence and power projections in the Indian Ocean. The increasing Chinese assertiveness has led to strategic alliances between US, India, Japan and Australia.

India, due its geopolitical compulsions, also depends on sea route for its energy needs. In this respect, Indian Ocean provides convenient accesses for trade, transportation of energy and communication. As India is rising, its economic development, commercial growth, political stability and national security are all dependent on the security of sea lanes and maritime security surrounding India. Around 55 percent of India's trade in Asia-Pacific transits through the South China Sea region (Liu, 2016). The growing energy demand has made India to connect with Asia-Pacific more comprehensively in order to ensure the region's maritime security.

The International Energy Agency's World Economic Outlook, 2015 projected India as the fastest energy demand state from 2014 to 2040. When India relies more on energy imports in the years to come, freedom of navigation in Indo-Pacific will have to be ensured. Indian navy will increase its presence in the Indo-Pacific to ensure the freedom of navigation. India's new maritime strategy sets Indian Ocean as the foreign policy priority. Therefore, India's objective is to maintain maritime dominance to counter China's expansionism in the Indian Ocean. Though both India and Taiwan may find it difficult to pursue an anti-China (for India) or anti-mainland foreign policy (for Taiwan), a cooperative context of understanding on China's rise in Asia can be a bounding factor between them (Pande, 2016).

In this area, Taiwan also has similar concerns. For up to 98.04 percent of its energy requirements, Taiwan relies on imports. In 2014, Taiwan depended on Middle East and Africa for meeting 50 percent of its energy requirements. Its 81.6 percent of oil supplies is from the Middle East. Therefore, for Taiwan also, Indo-Pacific region has become strategically significant for its development. But at the same time, due to the political difficulty of establishing official links with other powers along Indo-Pacific, there is a possibility that Taiwan will support the right of freedom of navigation and right of SLOCs.

As the mutual strategic interest generated by the emergence of Indo-Pacific increases, there is a growing need to review and reorient strategic planning on both the sides. Maritime security and energy security provides critical areas of cooperation between India and Taiwan. In this respect, India has been engaged in developing quadrilateral and triangular coalitions with US, Japan, and Australia to maintain regional security (Sandano, 2017). The insertion of Taiwan in this security structure can be a great advantage for both the countries.

In the Indo-Pacific geopolitical context, Taiwan's strategic location and sharing strategic interest with India would strengthen the route of common interest between the two sides. India's 'Act East Policy' can also play a proactive role by expanding the area of cooperation not only on economic, cultural and technological affairs, but also on strategic areas like maritime security and energy security. Forging military alliances is unrealistic and even Taiwan does not consider India as a military ally. But at the same time, Taiwan believes that the presence of India in East Asia as a balancer provides enough room for exercising its foreign policy choices judiciously.

Another area of strategic cooperation between India and Taiwan is the sharing of information. Taiwan knows China better than any other country in the world due to their historical, cultural, ethnic and linguistic ties. Taiwan has invested heavily in China studies, which can be used by India to understand what Chinese are saying and thinking about India. In 2013, the O.P. Jindal Global University provided a four week training programme in Mandarin language for Indian Army officers (Fang, 2016). The language course has helped the officers to acquire proficiency in Chinese language and thereby enhance communication with their Chinese counterparts. Later, some of these officers were deployed in the joint military exercises between India and China.

Economic Relations

The economic rediscovery between India and Taiwan was made possible largely by the structural changes brought about by global economic processes (Gopalan, 2016). The Taiwan government's New South Bound Policy converges with Modi government's 'Act East Policy' on deepening economic ties between the two countries. Given its huge foreign reserves and expertise in the field of hardware manufacturing, construction, infrastructure, mine exploration, electronic manufacturing, logistics, automobiles, food processing and others, Taiwan can play a vital role in the success of the Modi government's Make in India, Digital India and Skill India initiatives (Kumar, 2017).

Trade

Trade between India and Taiwan increased from US$ 1.2 billion in 2000 to US$ 6 billion in 2016 (Kumar, 2017). During the same period, India's exports to Taiwan increased from US$ 550 million to US$ 2.2 billion, while India's imports from Taiwan increased from US$ 640 million to US$ 3 billion. The total trade between the two sides grew from US$ 1.2 billion in 2000 to US$ 4.9 billion in 2015 (Yelery, 2016). India now ranks as the 16th largest export destination and 21st largest source of imports. As of 2016, about 90 Taiwanese companies are now working and investing in different sectors of the Indian economy. Their total investment reached at US$ 1.4 billion in the fields of information and communication technology, medical devices, automobile components, machinery, steel, electronics, construction, engineering, financial services etc. (TECC, 2017). Besides these initiatives, collaboration by small and medium enterprises between both the sides was also promoted. Even though, there was substantial increase in trade contacts, it is not impressive as it does not match with the potential. In this context, India can learn from Taiwan as to how to address the trade imbalance since Taiwan maintains surplus with mainland China (Fang, 2015).

Foreign Direct Investment

Taiwan is a small island country, having an outward looking economy, depending on global demand for economic growth. Taiwan enjoyed significant economic growth from the 1970 to 1990s, with a real GDP annual growth rate averaging about 8 percent (Hsu, 2016). It has also undertaken industrial restructuring by off shoring its labour intensive manufacturing industries to other low labour cost countries like China and Southeast Asia. Taiwan investment has resulted in the establishment of regional production networks and value added chains in the East Asian region. As a result, millions of jobs have been created across East and Southeast Asian states. It has resulted in a jump in Taiwan's economic growth in the early 1990s and the early 2000. According to the World Investment Report, 2015, published by UNCTAD, Taiwan's outward FDI flow in 2000 was US$ 66.66 billion. It increased systematically to US$ 258.83 billion in 2014 which is greater than Korea's outward FDI outflow.

But Taiwan's FDI inflow in India remained very low until 2000. Though the *Go South Pólicy* of Taiwan government was extended in 2000 to include India also, it did not produce any significant change. The Taiwanese companies conceded this inclusion as a complementary extension to the Southeast Asian States and not as a potential market for themselves (The policy was inaugurated in 1994 to encourage Taiwan's investment in Southeast Asian States). Compared to China and Southeast Asian states, Taiwanese investment in India is very low. Taiwan ranked only as the 37rd FDI source from 2000 to 2017 with an accumulated FDI inflow of US$ 287.02 million (Government of India, 2017).

But in August 2015, Faxconn Technologies, the world's largest electronic contract manufacturer from Taiwan announced a US$ 5 billion investment project over the 5 years to set up manufacturing and research and development facility in the western state of Maharashtra. This is the single largest investment project for the Narendra Modi's Make in India and Digital India initiative. The company also announced to invest US$ 500 million in India's e-commerce sector with Japan's Soft Bank and China's Alibaba. Faxconn's decision is based on India's huge market potential for smart phones and other electronic devices. India is expected to be the fastest growing smart phone market and may overtake US Smart phone market by 2017.

But at the same time, other leading Taiwan ICT companies like Wintek Technologies, D-Link, Synnex Tec, Asus Computers, Acer etc. has only limited presence in India in service, sales and distribution functions due to their low confidence in Indian manufacturing sector. They are very much concerned on issues like poor infrastructure, lack of adequate industrial foundation and very complicated central and state tax and legal system. For instance, Taiwan's Continental Engineering Corporation, involved in Delhi Metro Project, in 2013 complained of how it was being asked to seek prior approval for bringing capital each time under the RBI rules applicable to China (Singh, 2016).

In order to address these issues, there is a need for more collaboration between India and Taiwan in the ICT sector. Taiwan's experience, technology and technical knowledge in developing production network and global value chains are of strategic importance to India.

Cultural Relations

There is a good people-to-people contact between the two countries. In this respect, Buddhism served as a common bond of religious intimacy. India has also extended e-visa facility for Taiwanese to visit India. Besides this, in 2010, Taiwan decided to provide free visa entry to Indians who hold a valid visa of United States, Britain, Canada, Japan, Australia, and New Zealand.

Parliamentary delegation from Taiwan visited India under India-Taiwan Parliamentary Friendship Forum formed in 2016.

Educational Relations

In the educational field there are increasing opportunities for mutual collaboration. In 2017, there were 100,000 foreign students studying in Taiwan, of whom 1,310 students hailed from India (TECC, 2017). The Taipei Economic and Cultural Centre (TECC), New Delhi, has also established Mandarin centres in various Indian universities. Currently, there are 11 teachers from Taiwan teaching Mandarin, and there are over 3,000 Indian students who have taken Chinese courses in India (Hasija, 2017). In 2010, Foundation for International Cooperation in Higher Education of Taiwan signed a MoU with Association of Indian Universities, by which academic degrees and certificates recognized by one will be recognized by the other, allowing for greater research collaboration and exchanges by teachers and school administrators. Various Indian universities like India Institute of Technology, University of Delhi, Jawaharlal Nehru University in India and National Chiao Tung University, National Tsing Hua University and National Chengchi University in Taiwan offer exchange programmes. There are also mutual exchanges between strategic communities and think tanks and academics.

Conclusion

Even though there is limited understanding between India and Taiwan, there are several areas where the two countries can cooperate for mutual development. China is a major trading partner for India, but it should not in any way undermine its relations with any other state including Taiwan. If India aspires for great power status and greater role in international affairs it should change its conventional attitude towards Taiwan. India-Taiwan bilateral relations can be effective only if there is mutual understanding and passion for creative engagement between the two. In this respect, economic engagement can be a stepping stone upon which further relations in strategic security and military relations can be effectively built upon. The relationship with Taiwan therefore, in the long run can contribute to the realization of the strategic objectives of India's foreign policy.

References

Bush, Richard (2016), "The United States Security Partnership with Taiwan", Asian Alliances Working Paper Series, Paper 7, July, p. 2.

Fang, Tien-Sze (2015), "India-Taiwan Relations: A Comprehensive Security Perspective", *Indian Defence Review*, Vol. 30, Issue 4, October-December, p. 1.

Gopalan, T. Suresh (2016), "India and Taiwan: Emergence of an Economic Convergence", in Jagannath P. Pande (ed.), 'India-Taiwan Relations in Asia and Beyond: The Future', Pentagon Press: New Delhi, pp. 78-87.

Government of India, Ministry of Commerce and Industry (2017), "Quarterly Fact Sheet on FDI from April 2000 to December 2017", available at: http://dipp.nic.in/sites/default/files/FDI_FactSheet_21january 2018.pdf.

Hasija, Namrata (2017), "India Quietly Enhances Ties with Taiwan: Analysis", available at: https://www.eurasiareview.com/06022017-india-quietly-enhances-ties-with-taiwan-analysis.

Hsu, Kristy (2016), "India-Taiwan Economic Partnership in the Asian Era", in Jagannath P. Pande (ed.), 'India-Taiwan Relations in Asia and Beyond: The Future', Pentagon Press: New Delhi, pp. 69-77.

Jacob, T. Jabin (2016), "Taiwan-India Relations: Constrained or Self Constraining", in Jagannath P. Pande (ed.), 'India-Taiwan Relations in Asia and Beyond: The Future', Pentagon Press: New Delhi, pp. 37-47.

Kumar, Sumit (2017), "Trade Ties and Chinese Threat Brings India-Taiwan Closer", available at: http://www.dnaindia.com/analysis/column-trade-ties-and-chinese-threat-bring-india-taiwan-closer-2535578.

Liu, Fu-Kuo (2016), "Maritime Security and the Indo-Pacific Security Link: The Strategic Reorientation of India and

Taiwan", in Jagannath P. Pande (eEd.), 'India-Taiwan Relations in Asia and Beyond: The Future', Pentagon Press: New Delhi, pp. 101-109.

Pande, P. Jaganath (ed.) (2016), "India-Taiwan Relations in Asia and Beyond: The Future", Pentagon Press: New Delhi, pp. 1-7.

Pande, P. Jaganath (ed.) (2016), "India and Taiwan: Potential Regional Partners", in Jagannath P. Pande (ed.), 'India-Taiwan Relations in Asia and Beyond: The Future', Pentagon Press: New Delhi, pp. 56-68.

Sandano, Imran Ali (2017), "India's Dangerous Taiwan Gambit", *The Diplomat*, October 23.

Singh, Prashant Kumar (2014), "Transforming India-Taiwan Relations: New Perspective", Institute for Defence Studies and Analyses, Monograph Series No. 35, April, New Delhi, p. 70.

Singh, Prashant Kumar (2016), "Taiwan: The Forgotten Frontiers of India's Act East", in Jagannath P. Pande (ed.), 'India-Taiwan Relations in Asia and Beyond: The Future', Pentagon Press: New Delhi, pp. 19-36.

The Taipei Economic and Cultural Centre (2017), "Taiwan-India Relations', available at:

www.roc-taiwan.org/in-en/post/39.html.

Yelery, Aravind (2016), "India-Taiwan Economic Relations and the China Factor: Prospects of Synergies and Challenges for Regional Economic Integration", in Jagannath P. Pande (ed.), 'India-Taiwan Relations in Asia and Beyond: The Future', Pentagon Press: New Delhi, pp. 89-91.

Index

Index